PHOTOGRAPHY

PHOTOGRAPHY

Consultant Editors:
JONATHAN HILTON
BARRIE WATTS

A FIRST GUIDE
THE MILLBROOK PRESS
BROOKFIELD, CONNECTICUT

A Quarto Book

First published in the United States of America in 1994 by
The Millbrook Press Inc.
2 Old New Milford Road
Brookfield, Connecticut 06804

Library of Congress Cataloging-in-Publication Data

Watts, Barrie.
    Photography / Barrie Watts.
        p. cm.
    "A First guide."
    "A Quarto book" -- T.p. verso.
    Includes index.
    Summary: Beginning with an introduction to the different types of cameras and how they work, *PHOTOGRAPHY* goes on to explain how to take good photographs, and how to correct young photographers' most common mistakes.
    1-56294-735-4 (trade ed.) ISBN 1-56294-398-7 (lib. bdg.)
    1. Photography -- Juvenile literature. [1. Photography.]
    I. Title.
TR149.W38 1994
770'.23'3 -- dc20   94-6389
                                                                      CIP
                                                                      AC

This book was designed and produced by
Quarto Children's Books Ltd
The Fitzpatrick Building
188–194 York Way
London N7 9QP

ART DIRECTOR Louise Jervis
DESIGN Nigel Bradley
DESIGN ASSISTANCE Eileen Batterberry, Narinder Sahotay, Bernard Nussbaum
MANAGING EDITOR Christine Hatt
EDITOR Mandy Suhr
PICTURE MANAGER Dipika Parmar Jenkins
ILLUSTRATION Julian Baker

PICTURE ACKNOWLEDGMENTS
Key: a = above, b = below, l = left, r = right, c = center
Quarto Children's Books Ltd would like to thank the following for supplying photographs and for permission to reproduce copyright material. While every effort has been made to trace and acknowledge all copyright holders, we would like to apologize should any omissions have been made.

Ace Photo Agency/Mugshots, page 24cl, cr, bl, br. Rolf Richardson, page 46al. Mauritius, page 46cl. Peter Dazeley, page 46br. Lesley Howling, page 47cl. Gabe Palmer, page 47bl. Ronald Toms pages 48 ar, 62ar. Bruno Zarri, page 48bl. Geoff du Feu, pages 48br, bc. David Kerwin, page 49br. Simone Broadhurst page 51br. Nigel Bradley, pages 13ar, 33cl, 34ar, 39a, 50cl, br, 53al, bl, 59br, 63a, c, 65c, 81br. Paul Forrester/Quarto Publishing plc, pages 3br, 6bl, 10, 15b, 16a, 17cl, br, 18c, 28b, 30b, 36, 83, 84b, 87br. Michael Freeman, pages 25br, 25bl, 51l, 51ar. Fuji Photo UK Ltd, page 14a. C. H. Gomersall/RSPB, page 49cr, al. Jeremy Hilder, pages 7c, 18bl, c, 19ac, ar, b, 21b, 22b, 25cl, 26, 27, 29br, 33cl, 43ar, cl, br, 44cr, 45, 52ar, bl, 53ar, al, 58bl, 61bl, br, 62bl, 63b, 64ar, 65al, ar, 66br, 68a, 69a, 71c, b, 72, 73, 75, 80ar, cl. Mrs Margot Melmore/RSPB, page 49c. Helene Rogers, page 35cl. Barrie Watts, pages 14c, b, 15ar, 17a, 19al, ar, 20, 23, 24ar, 25al, ar, 32, 33a, br, 34, 35, 38bl, br, 42, 43al, 44br, 46ar, 54, 55, 56, 57, 58al, ar, br, 59al, ar, bl, 60, 61a, 65b, 66cl, 67a, b, 68b, 69b, 70a, 71ar, 74, 76, 77, 78, 79, 80br, 81a, bl, 84cl, 85, 86.
Front jacket photographs supplied by: Barrie Watts
Back jacket photographs supplied by: Barrie Watts (above right and left, below left), Jeremy Hilder (center right), Cannon (center left).
Manufactured by Eray Scan (Pte) Ltd, Singapore
Printed by Star Standard Industries (Pte) Ltd, Singapore

CONTENTS

GETTING STARTED

WHAT makes a great photograph? Read on and find out. In this section of the book, you'll discover everything you need to get started in your new hobby. Learn about the basics of photography and how the camera actually takes a picture. You'll find all the information you need to make the correct choice of camera and film, as well as simple technical explanations that will help you to get the very best out of your camera.

Often the most difficult part of taking a photograph is deciding *how* to photograph the subject you have chosen. This section covers the basic rules of composition, and provides lots of professional tips for creating exciting pictures. When you've finished your roll of film, you can follow the step-by-step guide to developing and printing your own photographs.

Don't forget that the best way to learn is by making mistakes. The simple "fault finder" at the end of this section will help you to identify exactly where you've gone wrong, so that you don't make the same mistakes again.

WHAT IS A CAMERA?

ALL cameras work in basically the same way. The camera body is a lightproof box. It has a lens at the front and a strip of light-sensitive film at the back that records an image. Light rays are reflected from the object you are photographing and enter the camera through the lens. This focuses the light to project a sharp image of the object onto the film. Inside the camera, before it reaches the film, the light passes through an opening called the aperture. This can be made larger or smaller, to control the amount of light that enters the camera. When you press the shutter-release button, the shutter, a barrier behind the aperture, opens for a timed period. As the shutter opens, the film is exposed to light and an image is recorded.

The combination of the amount of light the aperture allows through, and the length of time the shutter allows it to act on the film, controls what is called the exposure.

THE BIRTH OF PHOTOGRAPHY

For hundreds of years before photography was invented, artists used a drawing aid called a *camera obscura* meaning "darkened room." By making a small hole in the wall of a dark room, an upside-down view of the world would be projected onto the opposite wall. This could then be traced on-to paper or canvas.

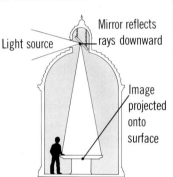

Light source — Mirror reflects rays downward

Image projected onto surface

An eighteenth-century camera obscura building.

Eventually, portable wooden *camera obscuras* were made and these looked a lot like the cameras of today.

In 1826, a Frenchman named Nicéphore Niépce used this principle to produce the first permanent images using the direct action of light.

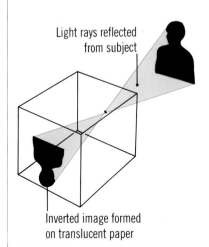

Light rays reflected from subject

Inverted image formed on translucent paper

You can make your own pinhole pictures using a lightproof box. The light from your subject enters the box through the pinhole and forms an upside-down image on the translucent paper.

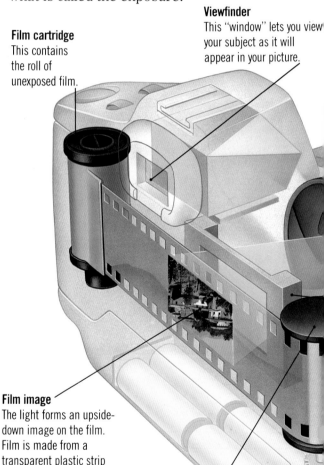

Film cartridge
This contains the roll of unexposed film.

Viewfinder
This "window" lets you view your subject as it will appear in your picture.

Film image
The light forms an upside-down image on the film. Film is made from a transparent plastic strip coated with chemicals called silver halides (compounds of silver). The silver halides change chemically when light falls on them, and in doing so, record the pattern of reflected light coming from the subject.

Take-up spool
Exposed film is wound onto the spool after each picture has been taken. When all the frames have been exposed, the whole film is rewound back into the cartridge and can be removed from the camera for processing.

Lens
Light enters the camera through the lens. The lens is a combination of specially shaped pieces of glass that bend, or refract, the light to form a sharp, focused image on the film.

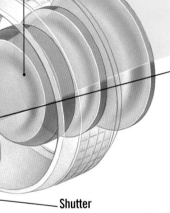

Light rays
Light rays are reflected from an object and enter the camera through the lens.

Aperture
The light passes through the aperture, a hole behind the camera lens: A circle of movable metal blades makes the hole larger or smaller. This controls how much light enters the camera, thus giving different amounts of exposure to the film. On simple cameras this is fixed at one size. On more complex cameras it can be adjusted. The aperture size may be controlled automatically or manually.

Shutter
The shutter opens when you press the shutter-release button, allowing light to reach the film. This controls when and for how long light is allowed to act on the film. Together with the size of the aperture, it determines the film exposure. The shutter is controlled either automatically, or by turning the shutter speed dial on a manual camera.

Changing views
With a compact camera, you look through a viewfinder window that is above and to one side of the lens. This means that there is a slight difference between what the viewfinder and the lens see. The SLR (single lens reflex) camera is different. Inside the SLR, a mirror angled at 45° reflects light from the lens up and out through the rear viewfinder window. This means that you always share exactly the same view as the lens, no matter what lens is used. When you press the shutter-release button, the mirror flips up out of the way and the shutter opens, allowing light to reach the film.

SLR viewing system

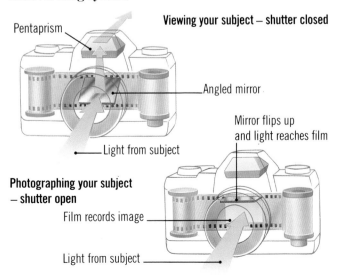

Viewing your subject – shutter closed

Pentaprism

Angled mirror

Mirror flips up and light reaches film

Light from subject

Photographing your subject – shutter open

Film records image

Light from subject

CHOOSING YOUR CAMERA

CHOOSING a camera can be a very confusing business! There are many different types and designs, all offering different features. They range from the simplest "point and shoot" cameras to very sophisticated models that are totally automatic, and even computerized. On the next few pages you will find a guide to the sorts of cameras that are available, starting with the least expensive, and an explanation of some of the most common features.

Fixed focus
This means that the lens cannot be altered to focus on subjects at different distances from the camera. It is preset so that everything from a few yards in front of the camera will be in focus.

Autofocus
This feature allows the camera lens to move in and out to focus automatically on any subject that you place in the target area of the viewfinder. You can focus on subjects closer to you than is possible with a fixed-focus camera.

Autoexposure
This means that the camera has a tiny cell that is sensitive to light falling on it from the subject. This cell automatically alters the aperture size or shutter speed, so the film receives the right amount of light for correct exposure.

Automatic (motor-driven) film advance
This means that the camera has a tiny motor that automatically winds the film on to its start position when you shut the back. It positions a fresh piece of film every time you take a picture, and then rewinds the film back into the cartridge.

110 cameras
These simple, inexpensive cameras have no controls, apart from the shutter-release button. Film comes in a drop-in cartridge. Each negative is very small and so enlargements can be poor quality.

Shutter-release button
Viewfinder
Lens

Shutter-release button
Built-in flash
Viewfinder
Lens

Shutter-release button
Viewfinder
Built-in flash
Lens cover control
Lens

Disposable 35 mm cameras

These are fun cameras with no controls. As they come loaded with 35 mm film, they give better-quality prints. When you have taken the last shot, you send the whole camera away for the film to be processed. Some models are waterproof or take long thin photographs called panoramas.

- *Fixed focus*
- *Simple autoexposure*
- *Built-in flash*

Simple 35 mm compact cameras

These take much better-quality pictures than either a 110 or a disposable camera, and allow you to change the speed of film that you use to compensate for bright or dim lighting conditions. These are easy to use cameras, ideal for quick "point and shoot" photographs.

- *Fixed focus*
- *Simple autoexposure*
- *Built-in flash*

Sophisticated 35 mm compact cameras

These cameras will take good-quality pictures of almost any subject, in most types of lighting. Some models give you a choice of two different lenses to use – a wide-angle lens for broad scenes or a telephoto lens for close-up pictures. Other models have a zoom lens, which starts off as wide-angle but, as you press a button, zooms into a telephoto.

● *Autofocus*

● *Good autoexposure*

● *Built-in flash*

● *Automatic film advance*

Zoom control button

Autofocus light receptor

Viewfinder

Built-in flash/red eye reduction lamp

Shutter-release button

Autofocus light projector

Self-timer/remote control lamp

Lens

Metering window

35 mm single lens reflex (SLR) cameras

SLR cameras are extremely versatile because you can take the lens off the camera body and fit on a different one. This means that with the right accessories you can tackle almost any kind of photography. Also, the scene through the viewfinder is always accurate. SLRs range from simple to very sophisticated models, and can be manually operated, fully automatic, or both. You can also attach a separate flash unit, which gives better lighting than the built-in flash.

● *Add-on flash unit*

● *Choice of autofocus, manual focus, or both*

● *Choice of different types of autoexposure*

● *Automatic film advance*

Viewfinder (behind)

Hot shoe

On/off switch

LCD panel

Camera strap eyelet

Focusing ring

Shutter-release button

Aperture control ring

Self-timer indicator

Lens

35 mm SLR system lenses and accessories

The range of lenses and accessories for 35 mm SLRs is vast. Most camera manufacturers have a system of lenses that fit the models they make, and these include lenses so wide that they see behind the camera, and telephotos so powerful that they can fill the frame with a picture of the moon.

Accessories include microscope adapters to take pictures of objects smaller than the eye can see and waterproof cases for underwater pictures of fish and coral.

▼ Camera body
You can buy a basic SLR body, without a lens, and then add your own choice of lens.

► Telephoto zoom lens
This comes in various focal lengths. It allows you to zoom in and take different-sized pictures of your subject from the same camera position by increasing the size of your image in the frame.

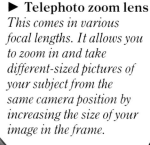

Lens-release button

Lens mount

► Wide-angle to short telephoto zoom lens
This versatile lens allows you to photograph broad scenes, as well as moderately close-up, detailed shots, without changing camera position.

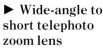

Attachment screw

Plunger

▲ Close-up lens
A focal length of about 75–135 mm is preferred by most portrait photographers. This will allow you to get close enough to crop out unimportant background detail, without distorting facial features.

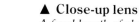

Adjustable flash head

Flash gun slides into hot shoe

▲ Cable release
This is an extension cable that allows you to release the shutter without touching the camera. You use a cable release, usually for a slow shutter speed, when it is important that you don't jar the camera.

UV filter

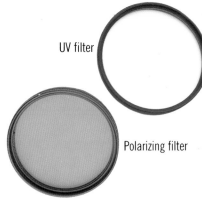

Polarizing filter

◄ Flash
You can attach a separate flash unit to all SLRs by sliding it into a special fitting on top of the camera called a "hot shoe." Some SLRs also have a built-in flash.

▲ Filters
Filters are colored discs that fit over the camera lens. They alter the way that light affects the film to enhance color or create special effects.

Built-in flash

Lens

6 3 6
closeup

Close-up lever

Shutter-release button (on side)

Lighten/darken control

Picture exit slot

Viewfinder

Instant-picture Polaroid cameras

Polaroid cameras are unlike any others because the film starts to develop as soon as you take the picture and is completely finished in about one minute. Although the pictures are instant, they are expensive per shot and the quality can be variable. The cameras range from very basic models to ones with automatic features.

- *Autofocus*
- *Autoexposure*
- *Built-in flash*

till video camera

The newest type of camera doesn't use film at all. Instead it uses a oppy disk, much like the type used in computers, to store your ictures. Prints can be made from the disk, but the camera is designed to show your pictures on an rdinary television set. It ses the same principles s a video camera, only the pictures are still. Once your pictures are on creen, you can record hem on your VCR and hen reuse the disk for ew pictures.

Fixed focus

Autoexposure

Built-in flash

Shutter-release/play button

Viewfinder

LCD display panel

Flash on/off button

Erase button

Date entry button

Floppy disk

Lens

Self-timer indicator

Built-in flash

Video signal output terminal

PROFESSIONAL CAMERAS

Professional photographers usually use large-format cameras when they are taking pictures in a studio. This is because the film they use is also large format, so the negatives are much bigger and pick up very fine detail, giving better-quality images. The lighting is controlled using special electronic flash lighting systems that can be finely balanced to give the exact amount of light needed.

WHICH FILM?

Film comes in a variety of types and sizes. The size of film that you will need to buy depends on the camera you have, but there are different types of film that can be used for most cameras. The type that you choose will depend partly on how you want your pictures to appear when they have been developed.

The most popular type of film is color negative, from which color prints are made. Black-and-white negative film is also available and gives black-and-white prints. If you want your pictures to be developed into slides for use in a projector, you will need to buy transparency, or slide, film.

Each type of film also comes in different speeds. You can tell the speed of a film by the ISO (International Standards Organization) number on the box. If you are going to be taking pictures in dull light you will need a fast film, such as ISO 400 or more. For bright light conditions, choose a slower film, such as ISO 100 or 200.

▲ **Instant pictur**
Polaroid film
Film for instant picture or Polaroid cameras comes in packs of individual sheets which are sel developing.

▼ **Size of film**
35 mm film is used for compacts and SLRs. 110 cameras and Polaroids use their own special films. You can buy larger format and sheet film for professional cameras.

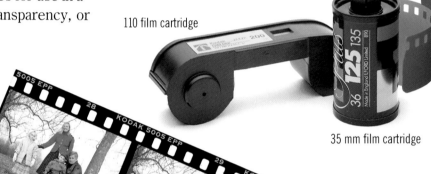

110 film cartridge

35 mm film cartridge

◀ **Color negative and print**
After processing, your color negative looks like this, with all colors of the original scene reversed. In fact, all the information is reversed, and th why it is called a negative. The negative is reversed again to produce a print.

18

FILM SPEED

The "speed" of a film refers to how sensitive it is to light. Faster films are coated with larger, lumpier grains of silver halides, which require less light to react. You should use a fast film when the lighting conditions for your photographs are poor, such as in dull weather. The higher the ISO number on the box, the faster the film is, and the more sensitive it is to light. For really poor light, you can even buy ISO 1600 or 3200, but you will find that pictures taken with very fast films tend to look quite grainy.

ISO 100 film

ISO 1000 film

◄ Coarse or fine?
Slow, fine-grain ISO 100 film (far left) records even small detail. Fast ISO 1000 film (left) gives a more grainy image.

▲ Color negative 110 film and print
Used only in 110 cameras, the negative is small. Prints need to be enlarged a great deal and consequently quality can be poor.

34   KODAK 5062 PX   35   KODAK 5062 PX   36   KODAK 5062 I

34   ▻ 34A   35   ▻ 35A   36   ▻ 36

▲ Black-and-white negative and print
A black-and-white negative has dark tones where the scene was bright, and light tones where it was dark. When the print is made, tones are reversed again, showing light and dark areas correctly.

Cardboard mounting

KODAK 5005 EPP

▲ Slide film
When you look at transparency or slide film, the scene looks just as it did when you took the picture. This is so that the pictures can be projected on to a screen or wall.

Plastic mounting

◄ Color slides
The film processor cuts your film strip up into individual frames and mounts each one in a cardboard or plastic holder ready for projection.

USING YOUR CAMERA

WHATEVER kind of camera you have, even if it's automatic, there are some simple basics you need to learn and understand so that you can use the camera effectively. One rule you should learn from the start is always to squeeze the camera's shutter-release button gently – never jab it, as this will give you shaky pictures. These pages contain information to get you started, but don't forget that you can also refer to your camera manual.

LOOK IT UP!
Aperture p. 13
Shutter p. 13
Depth of field p. 43, 88

Holding your camera

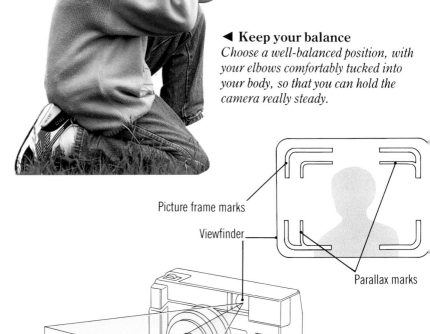

◀ **Keep your balance**
Choose a well-balanced position, with your elbows comfortably tucked into your body, so that you can hold the camera really steady.

▲ **Check your view**
Keep your fingers away from the lens. Check that the camera strap is also tucked well back before you take a picture.

Picture frame marks

Viewfinder

Parallax marks

View recorded by lens

View seen through viewfinder

▲ **Using a support**
If you need extra support for your camera, particularly when using a slow shutter speed, rest your camera against a solid object such as a tree or gate.

Using a compact camera
You must keep your subject within the corner marks of your viewfinder. But, because the viewfinder is above and to one side of the lens, there is a slight difference between what you see and what the lens sees. This is called parallax error, and it can result in your chopping off part of a close-up subject. To avoid this, make sure the important parts of your picture are within the extra parallax marks.

The SLR viewfinder

An SLR viewfinder has a central focusing aid, such as this split-ring. When the two halves of the circle are aligned, the image is correctly focused. A band around the split-ring, called a microprism collar, shimmers until the subject is in focus. A display in the viewfinder frame will indicate the shutter speed and aperture size that the camera's autoexposure has selected.

Shutter speed

The shutter speed helps to determine the amount of exposure the film receives. The speeds are marked in fractions of a second. Setting a shutter speed of $\frac{1}{125}$, for example, means that the shutter opens and allows light to reach the film for $\frac{1}{125}$ of a second. Each time you increase the shutter speed, you double the length of time the shutter remains open. The shutter also determines the precise moment that you take the picture.

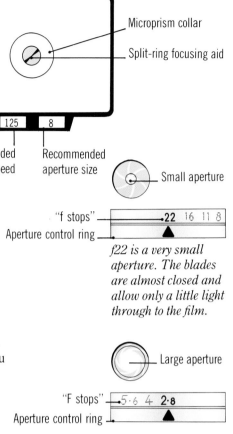

SLR viewfinder

Microprism collar

Split-ring focusing aid

125   8

Recommended shutter speed

Recommended aperture size

Small aperture

"f stops" — **22** 16 11 8

Aperture control ring

f22 is a very small aperture. The blades are almost closed and allow only a little light through to the film.

Large aperture

"F stops" — 5·6 4 **2·8**

Aperture control ring

f2.8 is a wide aperture. The blades open to allow lots of light through.

Lens aperture

The lens aperture works together with the shutter speed to determine the amount of light reaching the film. Aperture sizes are referred to as "f stops," and the larger the number of the "f stop," the smaller the size of the aperture. On most lenses, the apertures are f2, f2.8, f4, f5.6, f8, f11, f16, and f22, with f2 (and occasionally f1.8, f1.7, or f1.4) the largest size, and f22 the smallest. Each time you move down the scale, you double the size of the aperture, and so double the amount of light reaching the film. By balancing the size of the aperture with the shutter speed, you will select the right exposure. This will probably be done automatically by your camera, but sometimes you may wish to change the exposure manually. The numbers in the viewfinder display will blink or glow to indicate when you have selected the correct aperture to go with the shutter speed you are using.

HOW APERTURE SIZE AFFECTS FOCUS

As well as controlling film exposure, by letting more or less light into the camera, the size of the lens aperture also has an effect on the amount of the picture that is sharply focused. No matter where you focus the lens directly, there is always an area of your picture, both in front of and behind this point, which is also sharply focused. This band of focus is known as the depth of field. As you make the aperture size larger, the depth of field decreases, or becomes shallower.

Small aperture
A small aperture increases the depth of field, increasing the area around the subject that is sharply focused. If it is important that all the subject elements in your picture are sharp, use a slower shutter speed so that you can select a small lens aperture.

Large aperture
When the aperture is large, your subject will be the only sharp element in the picture. The depth of field will be very shallow. To create this effect, use the manual controls to select a large aperture. Use a faster shutter speed to correct the exposure.

COMPOSING YOUR PICTURES

GOOD photographs are not created just by skillful use of your camera; the most important skill is making an interesting choice and arrangement of objects within your picture area. This arrangement is called composition.

When you look through the viewfinder, think about what you want the focus of your picture to be. Will it be in the foreground or background of the picture? Look at your subject from different angles and spend time choosing your viewpoint. Consider the shapes, lines, and colors that you can see and look for something that will give your picture impact. By moving your camera position you may, for example, be able to include a brightly colored flower in an otherwise completely green field, or show the subject framed by trees.

You can pick up lots of tips from other people's pictures – in books, magazines, and newspapers. Keep a scrapbook of photographs that work well and use them for reference later.

▼ **Leafy landscape**
The smaller pictures (below) show less successful views of this landscape, tried out by the photographer before he took the picture on the right. They do not have an obvious main subject to tie the composition together.

▼ **City scene**
The picture below right is the most successful of these three cityscapes. By including the ship in the foreground, the photographer has given the city scene depth and scale.

▲ Unusual viewpoint
Even everyday things such as trees can make an interesting composition if you find an unusual viewpoint for your picture. This photographer lay on the ground on his back with the camera pointing directly upward.

Here the photographer has included the windmill as a point of focus. The strong lines of the path lead the viewer's eye to this point.

▲ Rural reflections
This striking landscape picture was made even better by balancing the mountains and hillsides with their mirror image, created in the calm waters of the lake.

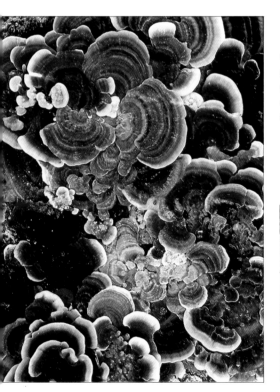

◄ Concentric circles
These fungi, taken in close-up using a macro lens, are a good example of the interesting compositions you can create by emphasizing natural pattern and texture.

LOOK IT UP!

Natural light
p. 24 - 25

Landscapes
and Cityscapes
p. 60 - 63

Macro lens p. 90

▲ Frames within frames
This picture has many layers. The outer frame is created by the photograph edges, the second by the honeysuckle, and the third by the window frame.

NATURAL LIGHT

OST photographs are taken using natural light. Because this light comes from the sun, it is constantly changing. The quality of light changes with the seasons, with the weather, and with the time of day. All these variations of light will affect the appearance of your photographs and the exposures needed for your film.

Most cameras automatically select the correct exposure, although many SLRs can also be operated manually. The speed of film you choose will also help to compensate for dull or very bright light. But you can use these varying types and angles of light to create different effects and atmospheres in your photographs.

▲ Early morning
As the sun rises in the sky, its low angle produces long shadows that give an image depth and texture. As the land is cold, the air can be very cool and clear, and this will give your picture a sharp quality.

Winter

Fall

Seasonal light
The landscape changes with the seasons, from spring when the trees bloom, to winter when they become bare skeletons of branches. But it also looks different because the sun's light changes as the seasons change. In summer, the sun is high in the sky and very intense. In winter, it barely climbs above the horizon, so it is far weaker. The light from a low sun has to travel through a great volume of atmosphere, so it is scattered. This creates a much softer lighting effect.

Summer

▲ ▶ Seasonal sights
These pictures show how a landscape can change dramatically as the seasons pass.

Spring

▲ Midday

At midday, light floods the landscape and its intensity can rob the scene of color and definition. As the sun moves overhead, shadows become short and very dense, increasing contrast dramatically.

▲ Evening

As the sun goes down in the evening, the light changes once again, giving a much softer appearance to the landscape. The low sun, directly behind the cactus, has produced a near-silhouette that looks very dramatic.

▲ Snowy scene

Snow and frost will often give your pictures a blue tinge because they reflect the ultraviolet parts of light.

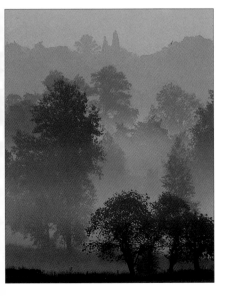

◀ Foggy weather

Fog and mist are more likely in early morning. They cling to landscapes, giving the light a hazy quality.

▲ Rainy weather

As this picture shows, rain can create a soft lighting effect, which can give your photograph atmosphere.

USING FLASH

YOU will need to use flash, or artificial light, in situations where there is not enough natural light reaching the film to expose it properly. Flash is almost always needed for indoor photography where the light is very limited. It is used out-of-doors in dull or evening light. Flash can be used in very bright light to reduce the contrast between light and dark areas of a picture. If you take a picture with the sun directly behind your subject (called backlighting), you can use flash to fill in the areas facing the camera that are in shadow.

Most cameras have a built-in automatic flash that is battery operated. SLRs, as well as sometimes having a built-in flash, have a special connector on top of the camera called a "hot shoe." This is where a flash unit can be attached to the camera.

When to use flash

Flash is ideal to use when there is not enough daylight in a scene indoors or outdoors. The color of the flash light is balanced for most color films, so the results will look natural.

▼ In the dark
If the subject is too far away from the flash when it fires, the scene will look unnaturally dark.

▲ Get it right
The flash must be the correct distance away from the subject to achieve the correct lighting results.

► Too close
If the flash is too close, the subject will appear bleached of color.

26

Direct flash

Flash (either built-in or an added accessory unit) pointed directly at the subject produces a stark, almost clinical type of lighting that can be quite unflattering. All of the subtle gradations of color or tone will be missing, and areas will be either lit or unlit.

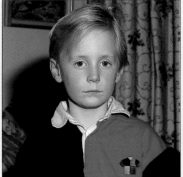

Diffused flash

Placing diffusing material (material that scatters light) such as a white handkerchief over the flash will soften the lighting effect and give a more flattering result. The distinction between lit and unlit areas becomes less obvious.

Bounce flash

If you use an SLR with an add-on flash unit, you can angle the flash head so that the light bounces off the ceiling or wall before reaching your subject. As the light is not direct, it is much softer.

Fill-in flash

Even when lighting levels are generally high enough to take a picture by natural light alone, there may still be occasions when you need to use flash. If the subject is backlit (left), for example, the side of the subject facing the camera will be very dark. To overcome this, you can direct the flash just into the shadow areas to brighten them a little (far left). This is known as fill-in flash.

DEVELOPING YOUR FILM

IF you have access to a darkroom, perhaps at school, you could try to develop your own black-and-white film to make negatives for printing. The technique described here is suitable for 35 mm black-and-white film only. Although the chemicals used in film developing are not very dangerous, you must always take care not to splash any of the concentrated chemicals on to your skin or in your eyes, especially since some of the time you will be working in total darkness. You may need an adult to help you.

How film is constructed

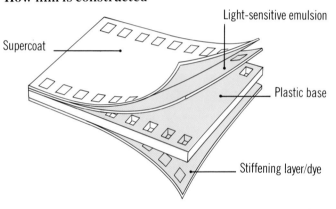

Supercoat

Light-sensitive emulsion

Plastic base

Stiffening layer/dye

A piece of film is constructed of many fine layers. The top layer of gelatine, known as a supercoat, protects the layers beneath. Under this is the important layer of light-sensitive emulsion, made up of millions of minute grains of silver-halide crystals. The thickest layer is the plastic base of the film, but there is also a stiffening layer to prevent the film from curling, as well as a layer of dye to prevent light reflecting back up through the emulsion from the film base.

Equipment

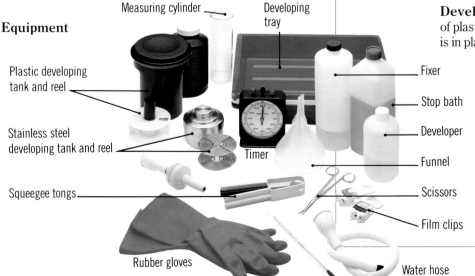

Measuring cylinder

Developing tray

Plastic developing tank and reel

Stainless steel developing tank and reel

Timer

Squeegee tongs

Rubber gloves

Thermometer

Fixer

Stop bath

Developer

Funnel

Scissors

Film clips

Water hose

Darkroom layout

The illustration below shows where the equipment in a well-organized darkroom should be positioned. For safety, the darkroom is divided into wet and dry areas.

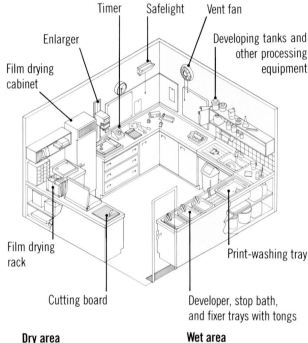

Timer

Safelight

Vent fan

Enlarger

Developing tanks and other processing equipment

Film drying cabinet

Film drying rack

Print-washing tray

Cutting board

Developer, stop bath, and fixer trays with tongs

Dry area
All "dry" processes are carried out on this side of the room.

Wet area
All "wet" processes are carried out on this side of the room.

Developing tank This can be made of plastic or stainless steel. Once the lid is in place, the chemicals can be poured in but no light can enter.

Chemicals The three chemicals you need are developer, stop bath, and fixer. The developer produces the negative; the stop bath halts the action of the developer; and the fixer dissolves unwanted silver halides and makes the film insensitive to light.

Step-by-step developing

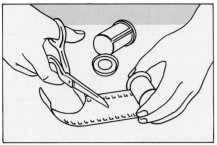

1 Arrange the developing tank and other equipment so you can find them in the dark. Turn out the light and open the top of the film cartridge. Slide the film spool out and cut off the shaped end of the film strip. Cut between sprocket holes to leave a clean edge.

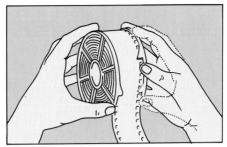

2 Load the film onto the reel and turn the reel slowly. Slightly bow the film, allowing the reel to pull it *loosely* through your fingers and onto the core of the reel. When you reach the end of the film, cut off the cartridge spool and tuck the last bit of film into the reel.

3 Put the loaded reel into the developing tank, fitting it over the center core. Put the lid on, securing it tightly. Now you can turn on the lights. Mix the developing liquid according to the manufacturer's instructions on the container.

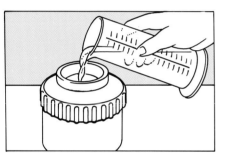

4 Remove the cap from the center of the lid and pour the developer in. Start the timer immediately and put the cap back in place. Rap the tank sharply on the edge of a hard surface to dislodge any air bubbles clinging to the film.

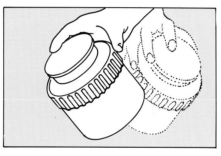

5 You must agitate the tank for 15–30 seconds during every minute of development, by constantly turning it upside down. After development, pour out the developer and pour in the stop bath. Agitate the tank for 30 seconds.

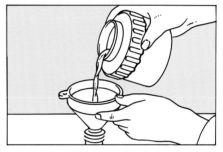

6 Pour the stop bath out and refill with fixer for the recommended time. The chemicals can all be reused a number of times. Pour them carefully into storage containers and note how many films they have been used to process.

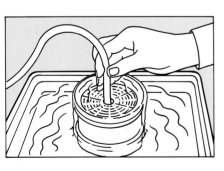

7 After removing the fixer, the film is developed and is insensitive to light. To remove all traces of chemical residue, take the lid off the tank and place the tank and reel under *gently* running *cool* water for at least 30 minutes. Too much water pressure may damage the still-soft emulsion.

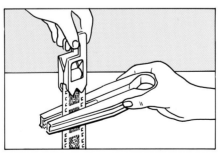

8 Wetting agent, added at the final washing stage, stops water droplets from marking the film. Carefully unwind the film from the reel and wipe it once with a clean pair of squeegee tongs. Attach a film clip to one end of the film and hang it in a dust-free area (a shower enclosure will work fine).

THE FINISHED NEGATIVE

Black-and-white negatives have dark tones where the scene was light, and light tones where the scene was dark. All the information is reversed, which is why they are called negatives.

Dark tones

Light tones

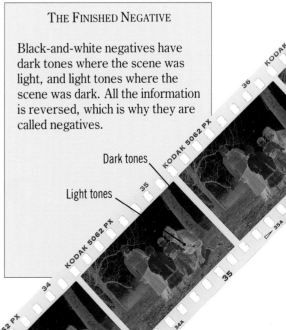

MAKING A PRINT

USING the negatives, you can make prints of your pictures. You will need to do this in a darkroom because the printing paper is also sensitive to most types of light. However, with black-and-white printing paper, you can work with a special red-colored "safelight" on at all times. But you must use only the recommended low-wattage lightbulb.

How a print is produced

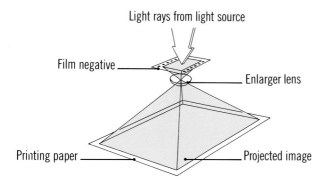

Light rays from light source
Film negative
Enlarger lens
Printing paper
Projected image

Only the clear areas of the film let light from the enlarger (right) through to the printing paper. Where the negative is black, the light is blocked; where it is gray, only some light can get through. The parts of the paper that receive light turn black, or a shade of gray, when developed. Areas that don't receive light remain white.

Because the tones of the subject were reversed as a negative and reversed again when printed, the finished print shows the original tones of the composition restored.

Equipment

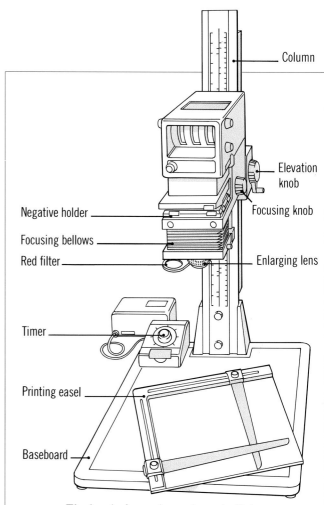

Column
Elevation knob
Focusing knob
Negative holder
Focusing bellows
Red filter
Enlarging lens
Timer
Printing easel
Baseboard

The head of an enlarger has a built-in light and a lens. Between the light and lens is a film carrier to hold negatives in position. Light travels through the film and into the lens. This can be focused until a sharp image appears on the baseboard below. The lens also has an aperture control to make the light brighter or dimmer for different negatives. The exposure time is controlled by turning the enlarger light on and off. A red filter swings over the lens to stop the light affecting the paper while you are focusing the image.

Photographic paper This comes in a variety of grades and surfaces. For your first attempts at printing, try grade 2 paper which is quick to process and dry.

Chemicals You will need developer to produce the image on the paper, stop bath to halt the developing process, and fixer to fix the image and stop any further chemical reaction.

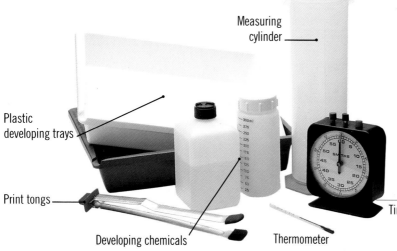

Measuring cylinder
Plastic developing trays
Print tongs
Developing chemicals
Thermometer
Timer

Step-by-step printing

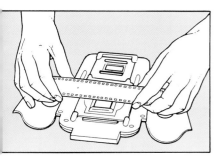

1 Cut the film into strips of six negatives. Place a negative into the film holder of the enlarger with the dull side facing down. Mix up the chemicals using the manufacturer's instructions, and pour them into separate trays.

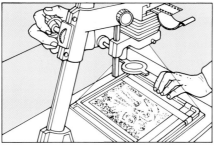

2 Turn the room lights out and the safelight and enlarger on. Adjust the height of the head until the image on the baseboard fits inside the edges of the printing easel, which should be set to the size of the paper you are using.

3 Focus the image using the focusing control on the lens. Set the aperture to the largest size, as this will give you the brightest image. Use a magnifier to check the focus of your image, and to make sure the negative is not distorted.

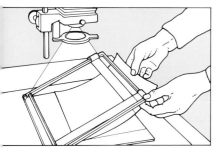

4 Swing the red filter over the lens. Position a piece of printing paper, shiny side up, in the printing easel. Check the focus, turn the enlarger off, and remove the red filter. Reduce the aperture by two stops to give a sharper result.

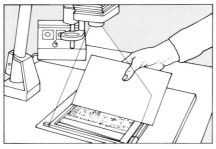

5 Make a test strip. Cover ¾ of the paper with cardboard. Turn the enlarger on and give a 10-second exposure. Move the cardboard to expose another strip for another 10 seconds, and so on. Continue until all the paper is exposed.

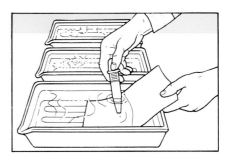

6 Slip the test strip carefully into the tray of developer. Rock the tray gently to make sure the solution reaches all of the paper's surface. Leave for the time recommended by the manufacturer's instructions on the container.

7 Use print tongs to remove the paper from the developer (allow excess developer to drain off) and place it in the stop bath. Agitate the stop bath for the recommended time. Using the other pair of print tongs, place the print into the tray of fixer.

8 After about 1 minute, remove the test strip print and wash it under running water. It will show strips of different exposure times. Decide which exposure is best (it may be between two strips – say, 25 seconds). Expose and develop a fresh sheet of paper to make your print.

9 Wash finished prints in clean running water for at least 30 minutes. This will remove all traces of chemicals. Change water in the washing tray continuously. Finally, dry your prints. If your paper is resin-coated, hang the prints up to dry, if fiber-based, lay flat.

FAULT FINDER

E VEN professional photographers with many years of experience make mistakes from time to time. This is always disappointing, especially if you can't easily take the picture again, but mistakes can be useful if you learn from them. Then you can avoid making the same mistakes in the future. This section of the book identifies many common errors, and explains how you can correct them.

Badly-framed subject – parallax marks ignored

Framing errors

Correct framing within parallax marks

What went wrong?
A compact camera was used too close to the subject and you ignored the viewfinder framing lines, or parallax marks.

What can I do?
Framing errors occur because compact cameras have a viewfinder separate from the lens. Make sure that you keep within the framing marks, and within the parallax marks for close-ups.

Lens obstruction

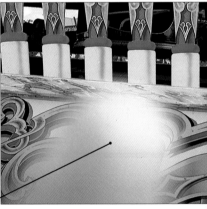

Finger intrudes into picture

What went wrong?
A finger, or part of the camera strap, was in front of the lens as the picture was taken.

What can I do?
This usually happens only with a compact camera because of its separate viewfinder. Before taking each picture make sure that your fingers, hair, camera strap, and any other possible obstructions are well away from the lens.

Camera shake

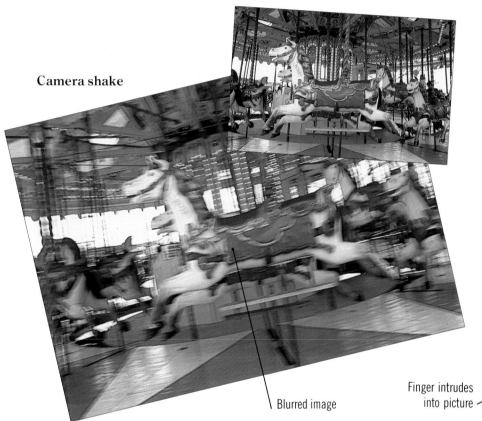

Blurred image

What went wrong?
The camera moved while you were taking the picture.

What can I do?
Always stand in a comfortable and balanced way, so you can keep the camera really steady. If possible, use a faster shutter speed (such as $1/125$ second), which makes camera shake less likely. Faster shutter speeds are also important with telephoto lenses. Because these lenses are heavy, even slight camera movement shows up. If you have to use a slower speed, support the camera on a firm, even surface, and always press the shutter-release button gently.

Central target area
ignored when focusing

Correct target
area for focusing

Focusing errors

What went wrong?
With an automatic camera, the subject was probably not in the central target area used by the autofocus system to focus the camera. On a manual camera, you did not set the focusing controls on the lens accurately.

What can I do?
With an automatic camera, pay attention to where the subject is located in the viewfinder. On a manual, check the focusing screen carefully before shooting.

Vignettes

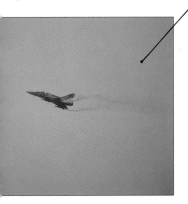

Dark area
around image

Lens flare

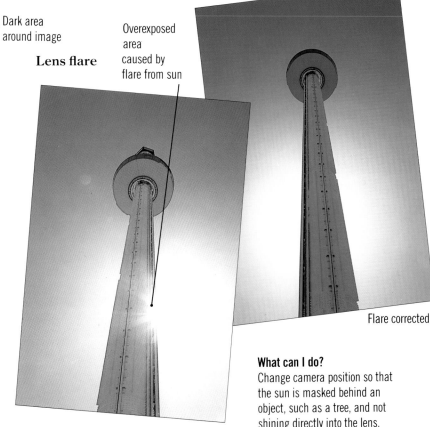

Overexposed
area
caused by
flare from sun

Flare corrected

What went wrong?
The edge of the picture has been obscured. There appears to be a dark area, or vignette, surrounding part of the image.

What can I do?
This only occurs on SLRs. The most likely cause is that a lens hood, designed for a standard or telephoto lens, was used on a wide-angle lens, or zoom set to wide-angle. Sometimes a vignette is also caused when a polarizing filter is fitted to the lens, as this has a double-depth rim.

What went wrong?
The picture was taken with the lens pointing directly at the sun.

What can I do?
Change camera position so that the sun is masked behind an object, such as a tree, and not shining directly into the lens. This should eliminate the flare while keeping the same lighting effect on the subject.

Abrasions

Abrasion

What went wrong?
The film surface is very delicate and it has been scratched, probably by grit inside the camera.

What can I do?
Make sure that the inside of your camera is completely clean, particularly the film pressure plate on the inside of the camera back. Nothing can be done to correct scratches after they have occurred.

Overlapping frames

Overlapping double image

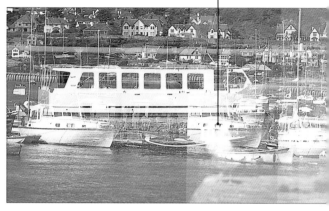

What went wrong?
The most likely cause is that the film was not properly loaded and consequently has not wound on after each picture was taken.

What can I do?
Follow the instructions in your camera manual for loading film. Usually the camera has a system that allows you to check that film i· winding on properly. You will also find this in the manual.

Flash exposure problems

Correct

Too light – highlights bleached

What went wrong?
The flash was either too close or too far from the subject when fired.

What can I do?
Make sure you are the correct distance from your subject (check your manual for distances). Flash light reduces in intensity as it travels. This limits you to taking pictures within about 10 ft (3 m) of your subject. This isn't a problem indoors, but outdoor subject distances are often greater. Get closer to your subject or use a faster film. Overexposed flash pictures are caused by being too close or by using an aperture that is too wide. Read the flash manual to find the correct aperture for each subject distance.

Fogging

What went wrong?
Until film is fully processed it remains sensitive to light. Any stray light reaching the film will make the image "misty."

What can I do?
This orange "veil" is typical of film that has been exposed to light other than that from the lens. Make sure that you load a new film away from bright light, and that you rewind the film completely into its cartridge before removing it from the camera. You cannot correct this problem after it has occurred.

Orange "veil"

Too dark – background detail dense

Flash synchronization

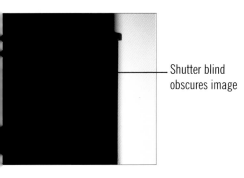

Shutter blind obscures image

What went wrong?
This problem is confined to SLRs and is caused when the flash fires before the shutter is fully open.

What can I do?
With an SLR, you must set the shutter to the correct speed for flash synchronization – usually $\frac{1}{125}$ second – or to the lightning flash symbol. Check your user's manual. If you have done this and the problem persists, the camera will need to be taken in for repair.

Red eye

Red spots in eyes

What went wrong?
Because the flash is close to the camera lens, the light has reflected back from the blood vessels in the subject's eyes.

What can I do?
This problem is most common on compact cameras, although many now are fitted with an anti-red eye flash device. If you can't add a flash unit or bounce the light, as with an SLR, ask the subject to glance away from the camera as you take the picture.

Processing errors

Correct color balance

Too much blue

Too much yellow

What went wrong?
Color errors affecting all of the prints, such as those shown here, are likely to have been caused during processing.

What can I do?
If the negatives are not affected, take bad prints back to the processor (with the negatives) and ask for a free reprint.

FAULT FINDER

LOOKING
AND LEARNING

Now that you have learned how your camera
works and how to use it, it's time to go
out and take some pictures. This part of the
book is divided into projects, each
one covering a different subject area.
The projects are designed to show you the wide
range of picture opportunities available, as well
as different techniques you can use to create
unusual compositions and special effects.
You will learn how to take portraits of people
and photograph animals and nature.
Landscapes, cityscapes, and buildings provide
plenty of scope to practice your photographic
skills. Techniques for capturing movement are
covered on the sports and action pages.
There is information on lenses and setups
needed for still life and close-up photography.
You can also learn how to play around with
images to make abstract designs, montages, and
panoramas, and to create unusual lighting effects.

PEOPLE PORTRAITS

Most people buy their first camera to take pictures of family and friends, so a portrait will probably be one of the first photographs you take. Before you take the picture, think about the type of image you want. You can ask people to pose for you, but some of the best pictures happen when the subject doesn't know that a picture is being taken. This type of informal picture is called a candid photograph. For posed portraits, it is a good idea to take lots of pictures to help your subject overcome any shyness.

Choose your background and camera angle carefully and decide what will be best for the type of shot you want. If you are using a camera with a wide-angle lens, such as a simple compact, remember that moving in very close may distort your subject's features. A zoom lens of about 90 mm is excellent for portraits.

▲ **Posed potrait**
Portraits are usually thought of as formal, posed pictures, such as this photograph.

◄ **Simple shots**
Simple, candid shots are very effective and can be taken easily with a telephoto lens or zoom. This allows you to stand well back, so the subject is not likely to notice the camera.

LOOK IT UP!
SLR lenses p. 15, 91
Parallax error p. 20
Self-portraits p. 80–81

◄ **Tips on candids**
If you don't want your subject to know you are taking a picture, you will have to blend into the background as much as possible. Use a zoom lens, and preset the focus and exposure controls so that you will be ready to shoot when your subject is naturally distracted. You may need to support the camera if you are using a heavy lens.

◀ ▼ **Using longer lenses**
Telephoto or zoom lenses allow you to close in and capture facial expressions when you are taking candid shots, such as the collection on this page. All of the subjects were engrossed in what they were doing and totally unaware of the photographer. Shots such as these often tell a lot more about the person being photographed than posed pictures.

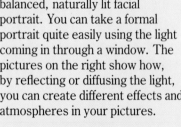

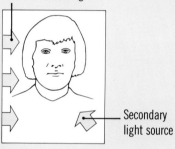

Direct window light

Area in shadow

The subject is positioned so that her face is lit by direct window light. However, as the light is only coming from one direction, one side of her face is in shadow.

The picture above shows a well-balanced, naturally lit facial portrait. You can take a formal portrait quite easily using the light coming in through a window. The pictures on the right show how, by reflecting or diffusing the light, you can create different effects and atmospheres in your pictures.

Using daylight film indoors

Direct window light

Secondary light source

The photographer has added a secondary light source, directed at the right side of the face, to soften the shadowed area. But the effect is still quite harsh.

Using normal daylight-balanced film with indoor electric lighting will give your pictures a warm, orange cast. This can be a flattering lighting effect.

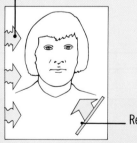

Diffused window light

Reflector

By covering the window with white mesh or cloth, the light is diffused, or scattered. This gives a softer and more flattering lighting effect. By adding a reflector, the shadows are further softened.

▼ ▶ Group portraits

The more people there are in a picture, the more difficult it is to arrange them so they can all be seen. Choose the background carefully, then organize the group so that the tallest are at the back and smallest in the front. This is particularly important for a formal group shot (below), but even in a simple group lineup (right), you still need to be able to see all the faces.

LOOK IT UP!

Flash
p. 26 – 27

Natural light
p. 24 – 25

Daylight-balanced
film p. 88

▼ Family faces

This family group is a much more relaxed shot. Although the subjects have not been formally arranged, they are posing directly for the camera.

ANIMAL PORTRAITS

GOOD animal photographs can be tricky to take. You cannot direct animals to pose for you as people do, so you need lots of patience.

The easiest animal subject to use is a pet and it is best to photograph your pet outside, as flash might frighten it. For an active type of animal, such as a dog, you could try taking some action photographs. Think carefully about how you compose your pictures, and experiment with unusual viewpoints and camera angles. You could even get in close for a dramatic view that perhaps does not show all of the subject.

Take a trip to a zoo or wildlife park for pictures of more unusual animals. If you call beforehand you may be able to find out the feeding times and take some really exciting shots!

GETTING THE EYELINE RIGHT

◀ From above
Many people take pictures of their pets looking down on them from a standing position. But, because the camera is above the eyeline of the animal, it is difficult to capture its character.

◀ At eye level
This picture was taken with the camera at the same level as the dog's eyes. By looking directly into the animal's face, the picture communicates much more of the dog's individuality.

▲ Dramatic angle
For this portrait, the photographer used a wide-angle lens, moved in close, and took the picture from below.

LOOK IT UP!

SLR lenses p. 15, 91

Depth of field p. 21, 88

◀ **Filling the frame**
This photograph of a peacock was taken in a wildlife park. The bird was used to visitors and very tame. It allowed the photographer to get close enough to fill the viewfinder.

▲ **Feeding animals**
You can use a small amount of food to encourage your subject to come in closer to the camera, like this squirrel. But never feed animals at a zoo.

...*(most cameras will then automatically correct the exposure). As you focus, you will see in the viewfinder that the wire seems almost to disappear. This is because of the shallow depth of field of wide apertures on telephoto lenses. Although the subject will be in focus, the background will not, and the wire will be so out of focus that it will appear almost transparent (right).*

SPORTS AND ACTION

THERE are two ways you can give your pictures a real sense of movement – that is either by "freezing" or "blurring" the action. For both of these you will need to be able to alter the shutter speed on your camera. On an SLR, you do this by moving the shutter speed dial. The aperture size will then need to be changed to give the correct exposure. Most compact cameras do not allow you to change the shutter speed manually, but by altering the speed of the film, you can often get the autoexposure to select a fast or slow shutter speed.

To freeze action, select a fast shutter speed. This means that the shutter will only open for the briefest instant, so won't record the subject moving. With an automatic camera, take pictures in bright light and on fast film, and the autoexposure will select a fast shutter speed.

To create "blur," use a slow shutter speed so the subject moves while the shutter is open. With an automatic camera, shoot in poor light on slow film, and the autoexposure should then select a slow shutter speed.

Other techniques include "panning" the camera and using flash. If flash is your main source of light, such as at night, it will freeze movement because the burst of light lasts for only a fraction of a second.

▲ **Mixed techniques**
This exciting action picture is the result of mixing flash with a slow shutter speed and exaggerated camera movement.

◀ **Fast shutter speed**
For this picture the photographer used a shutter speed of 1/500 second, which was fast enough to freeze even the fastest-moving part of the subject – the bicycle wheels.

▲ **Slow shutter speed**
If you choose a slow shutter speed, such as 1/15 second, with a moving subject you will get a blurred effect. But remember that with a slow shutter speed you need to support the camera to keep it perfectly still.

▶ **Flash and daylight**
Using flash in daylight means that you will increase the contrast between the subject, which will appear very bright, and the background, which will appear much darker.

Capturing movement

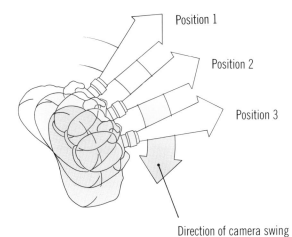

Position 1

Position 2

Position 3

Direction of camera swing

Position 1

Position 2

Position 3

▲ Pivoting the camera

The diagram (above) shows how the pictures on the right were taken. Using a fast shutter speed, the photographer changed the position of the camera by pivoting it to line up with the subject at three separate points. Although the photographer has captured the moving subject, there is very little feeling of action in the image. Compare this with the panned photograph (below), which has a greater sense of movement.

◄ Action panning

Panning means swinging the camera in an arc to keep up with a moving subject. For this to be effective, you need to select a shutter speed suitable for the speed of your subject. For example, with a running figure a shutter speed of about 1/30 second should "blur" the still parts of your picture while giving you a sharp image of the subject. With this racing car, you would have to pan the camera much faster, so a shutter speed of 1/250 second is more appropriate. The background will still "blur" because the camera is moving a lot faster to keep up with the subject.

▲ ► Canoe views

These two pictures, both of canoeists in action, show how important it is to think carefully about the viewpoint you choose. Action pictures are often more exciting if the subject is large in the frame. Get as close as you can to the action or use a telephoto or zoom lens.

▲ ► Changing views

If your camera allows you to alter the shutter speed, you can photograph the same subject in different ways. Choose a fast speed for "frozen" action pictures (above) or a slow speed for more atmospheric pictures (right).

◄ Toboggan tracks
This picture is simple but effective because the photographer has used a low viewpoint to emphasize the pile of snow in front of the tobogganist, and the tracks made as he traveled down the slope.

▼ Speeding skateboarder
Although the background is blurred, the skateboarder is frozen because he is lit mainly by the burst of light from a flash.

▼ ► Peak of action
This is a perfect moment to capture on film. The skateboarders are balanced at the peak of action, ready to hurtle downward.

NATURE SAFARI

YOU don't have to be in the country to photograph nature. You can find many different types of wildlife in the most ordinary places. In fact, you can discover unexpected creatures in towns and cities. In your garden, local park, or in empty lots, you can find a wide range of different plants and flowers. If there is water nearby, you may spot amphibians, such as frogs, toads, and newts, as well as different species of birds and small animals. If you learn a little about their habits – such as where and when they like to feed – you will find it easier to capture some of these animal subjects on film. By setting up a feeder in your garden, you will find that your subjects come to you.

You can use a compact camera with zoom ability for many nature pictures, but to magnify subjects such as flowers or completely still animals, you will need to use an SLR or sophisticated compact that has a macro lens setting. A telephoto lens or zoom is also very useful because it means that you can stand well back from your subject so you don't frighten it, but still get a reasonably large image in your viewfinder.

▲ Captured
To get a close-up effect with a compact camera, use a zoom if you have one, or get as close as you can then have part of the shot enlarged by the processor.

LOOK IT UP!
SLR lenses p. 16, 90, 91
Animal portraits p. 42 - 43
Macro lens p. 90

▲ Run rabbit run
This photographer used a telephoto lens with a focal length of 200 mm to close in on a rabbit.

▲ Close-up color
To focus on a subject less than 3 ft (1 m) from the camera, such as this colorful butterfly, you will need to use an SLR or compact that has a macro setting.

▲ Froggy features
To get really good close-up nature shots, you will need to be very patient. Rest your camera against a support and be ready to shoot at just the right moment.

▼ Feeding time
If you hang a feeder near a window, you will be able to get close to your subjects without their seeing you.

If you want to encourage birds and small mammals into camera range, provide your potential subjects with a reliable source of food and water. Birds not only like bread, nuts, and seeds, but many also enjoy scraps of meat and fat, especially in winter when food can be difficult to find. Any mammals not in hibernation will also appreciate your gesture. When it is very cold, leave plenty of water out in shallow bowls, because most natural water supplies may be frozen over. If you set up a bird feeder, make sure it is located where you will have easy access with your camera and plenty of natural cover to hide from your subjects.

▲ Collecting cones
You can collect seeds, cones, and berries to make your own bird feeders.

▶ Winter weather
If you put food out in snowy weather, you can guarantee that birds will stop for a welcome meal.

PHOTOGRAPHING BUILDINGS

THE many types and styles of buildings, from ancient cathedrals to giant skyscrapers, offer endless opportunities for interesting photographs. You can take pictures of unusual details, such as doorways or windows, but if you want to photograph the whole structure it can be quite difficult to get far enough back. This is where a wide-angle lens is useful, as it allows you to photograph a larger area.

Even with a lens like this, you may have to point the camera up to avoid cutting off the top of a building. Although this distorts the image, creating an effect known as "converging verticals," this distortion can add impact to the photograph.

LOOK IT UP!

Cityscapes p. 62 - 63
Natural light p. 24 - 25
Wide-angle lens p. 16, 91
Composition p. 22 - 23

SLOPING VERTICALS

Taken from ground level with the camera pointed upward, the sides of tall buildings seem to point inward, or converge.

A solution is to move farther back, so that you don't have to angle the camera upward, and use a telephoto lens for a larger image.

◀ **Simple shrine**
Although the building was not really attractive, this pretty shrine set into a wall made an effective detail shot.

▶ **Doorway detail**
Evening light, when the sun is low in the sky, was ideal to pick up the rich textures and colors of brick, wood, and stone in this medieval Italian street.

◀ Mirror image
This unusual composition captures the image of one building in the mirrored-glass wall of another. The reflection is made even more interesting because of the way the image of the building has been distorted. The photograph also contrasts two completely different architectural styles in one image.

▲ Dramatic angle
This stunning composition of an already dramatic building was taken in early evening. The warm tones of the light emphasize color, and the unusual camera angle emphasizes height.

▲ Around the house
Don't forget that you can photograph your own home. If you compose the picture carefully and choose an interesting viewpoint, you can show something seen every day in a completely different way.

I LIVE HERE

YOU can use your camera to record a personal view of your own home, told through the pictures you take of your favorite things, family, and friends. Photograph your toys, books, and pets, or just a corner of a room that tells a story. Include pictures of people in your collection, maybe in situations that you see regularly.

We often take for granted the things we see every day, so look very carefully at familiar surroundings. Take some close-up pictures. You will find that they often bring to light small features that you wouldn't normally notice. Make use of any interesting lighting, such as sunlight coming through a window.

► Candid camera
This is the photographer's sister sitting at her desk as she does every day.

LOOK IT UP!
Natural light p. 24–25
Still life p. 70–73
People portraits p. 38–41

▲ Bedroom clutter
Don't straighten up your room for this project. It's supposed to show things as they really are – mess and all.

▲ Hide-and-seek
A telephoto lens captured a friend in the garden in the middle of a game of hide-and-seek.

◄ Posing people
You can take posed pictures, like this one of two young friends, as well as more natural shots.

▲ Green thumb
The photographer grew all the plants and seedlings shown here.

▲ Toy friends
The photographer's collection of toys, arranged on a bedroom shelf, is a perfect subject for this project.

◄ Glowing globe
This globe is one of the photographer's favorite possessions. When illuminated, it creates an interesting lighting effect.

PHOTO STORY

A PHOTO story is a detailed, informative series of pictures. They are usually created by photo-journalists, who record events purely through photographs. The pictures may show an occasion or activity, or record the daily routine of someone who has an interesting occupation.

For this project you will become a photo-journalist. Choose a subject you are interested in or record a day in the life of someone you know. This photographer followed a fly fisherman for a day and, like a photojournalist, experimented with different camera angles and positions to create a varied collection of different shots.

Your final pictures should tell the viewer all about the events that you have photographed, without needing any words at all.

▼ Setting the scene
This attractive landscape establishes the scene for the whole activity by giving it a background setting. It gives further information by showing the special waterproof clothing the fisherman wears to wade into the river.

▲ Fishing tackle
Most experienced fly fishermen make their own flies. These are insect-shaped lures that attract the fish to the hook. This opening shot is full of interesting detail, which captures the viewer's attention. It immediately outlines the difference between this and other types of fishing, and invites the viewer to find out more.

▲ Detailed activity
This shot focuses in on the fisherman's hands as he attaches a fly to his line. Although you cannot see his face, you get a sense of the concentration involved.

▲ Camera close-up
To get just the right image, you will have to experiment with camera angles and positions. This close-up shows in detail the flies the fisherman has created.

▶ The punchline
Every good story – in words or pictures – needs to have a punch at the end. The obvious way to conclude coverage of a day's fishing expedition is with a picture of a fish in the fisherman's net. The photographer took the picture from directly overhead, giving the impression of looking straight into the net.

LOOK IT UP!

| People portraits p. 38–41 |
| Close-ups p. 76–77 |
| SLR equipment p. 16 |
| Still life p. 70–73 |

VACATION PHOTOGRAPHS

VACATIONS are the perfect time to practice your photography. You can discover many colorful and exciting subjects when you visit a new place. Use your camera to record images of different lifestyles, interesting architecture, and unusual shops and markets. A panorama could be used to record a stunning view, and you should find opportunities for some candid shots.

Don't load yourself down with too much equipment. A camera with a zoom lens is ideal because it can take wide views as well as detailed close-ups. If you are going somewhere sunny and hot, you can take a slower ISO 100 film.

VACATION PHOTOGRAPHY CHECKLIST

● Keep equipment to a minimum.
● Don't leave your camera in hot sunshine for long periods, or the film may be ruined.
● When you are at the beach, make sure that sand doesn't get into the camera – it can jam the inner workings or scratch the lens.
● Look for details of buildings, such as windows and doors, to give variety to your photographs.
● Take candid shots in markets, or action shots if you visit a beach or pool.
● Get up early to capture local atmosphere and color when shops and markets prepare for the day.

◀ ◀ ▲ **People watching**
You should find lots of opportunities for candid shots like this (left). But if you have time, and your subjects don't object, try taking a more considered, informal portrait (above and far left).

◄ ▲ Display details

When you visit new places, look for displays of unusual subjects. Move in close to take the picture and crop out all the surrounding detail to add impact to the composition.

▲ ► Getting in close

Close-up shots such as these emphasize color and shape. Street markets are an excellent source of close-up and still life subjects (right). In the countryside, look for colorful scenes like this field of giant sunflowers (above).

▲ Earth bound
Look downward – unusual paving or parched earth like this is a perfect subject for an abstract image. It will provide an unusual textural reminder of your vacation.

▲ Instant sunshine
Look for interesting detail on houses and other buildings. This scene of flowering plants against a rough, sun-baked wall and tiled roof is full of Mediterranean sunshine.

▶ Off the wall
If you see a group of likely subjects, such as these men sitting on a wall, don't hesitate to take a quick candid shot.

▼ Furry friends
Animals can also provide reminders of your vacation. This black-and-white study is of the hotel owner's cat.

▶ In the country
Pictures of the surrounding countryside can reveal another aspect of the place you have visited. This well-balanced composition is bursting with strong, natural colors, and the swans provide a perfect point of focus.

▼ ▶ Dramatic duo
*In both shots, picture shape complements
the subject. Below, the emphasis is on the
converging verticals of the building. The
waterfall (right) is framed by trees.*

▼ Seashore studies
*These simple studies give a real feeling
of the seashore. This seagull (below left)
was snapped with a telephoto lens. The
boy (below) was perfect for a candid shot.*

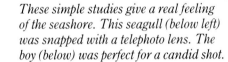

LANDSCAPES AND CITYSCAPES

APART from photographs of family and friends, landscapes are one of the most popular subjects for the camera. An impressive landscape can make a great picture, and there are plenty of different locations to choose from. Country landscape scenes can range from a patchwork of fields to snowy mountain peaks. Parks and nature reserves offer plenty of opportunities, too. But landscapes also include city views – often called cityscapes – and these can be just as dramatic.

Natural light plays an important part in landscape photography. The sun moves through the sky during the day, creating a variety of different lighting effects. A good time for landscape photographs is often in the early morning or the late afternoon. At these times of day the sun is low in the sky and the angle of its light tends to make colors look darker and richer. The landscape seems to be full of interesting shadows and textures. Light also alters with the seasons and with the weather, so these will change the appearance of the landscape, too. One of the secrets of successful landscape photography is always to keep one eye on the weather and the other on the clock. Be ready to photograph a favorite scene when you think the conditions are right. Bad weather doesn't necessarily mean bad photographs; some of the very best landscape pictures have been taken in stormy weather – but usually not when it's actually raining.

POSITIONING THE HORIZON

The horizon line is where the sky meets the land. In most landscape photographs you can see the horizon. Part of creating a good composition is deciding where it should be in your picture. If you point the camera down, the horizon appears near the top of the frame (1). This makes the picture look closed in, and also gives you a lot of foreground. If you point the camera up, the horizon is toward the bottom of the frame (2). This shows a lot more sky and gives a feeling of space in the photograph. Both of these are more dramatic images than the final picture (3), where the horizon is in the middle of the frame.

1. High horizon line

2. Low horizon line

3. Mid horizon line

▲ Stormy light

In this picture the lines of hills on either side of the trees guide the eye toward them. Their strong, bleak shapes are an important part of the composition. The photographer waited for the sun to shine through the storm clouds before he took the picture.

◄ ▲ Moving water

Moving water, such as fountains or waterfalls, can either be recorded with a fast shutter speed, so that its motion is "frozen," or a slow speed, so that the water blurs while the picture is being taken. In the first picture (left) a shutter speed of 1/500 second was used, and in the other (above) a shutter speed of 1/15 second was used, with the camera held on a tripod to keep it steady.

Knowing what will be the best lighting for your chosen scene is just as important for town and city photographs as for country landscapes. These "cityscape" pictures are just as rich in interest, color, tone, texture, and pattern as their country counterparts. It is the quality and direction of light that emphasizes or tones down all of these aspects. The sky is one of the most important elements in a landscape or cityscape shot. Early in the morning, or toward dusk, when the sun is not far above the horizon, the sky can be full of fabulous fiery colors, and clouds can look extremely dramatic. A sky like this, seen above the silhouetted shapes of tall city buildings, perhaps with low sunlight glinting off a few high windows, could be a terrific photograph.

Early evening or night photography is also interesting to explore. Once shop windows, car headlights, and streetlighting are lit up, an ordinary scene can be transformed into a fantasy image. You can make these light sources produce strange colors and distortions using normal daylight-balanced film, or you can pan the camera to achieve a sense of movement and action. As the night sky becomes darker, you will almost certainly need a tripod or some flat surface to steady the camera during exposure times that could last for many seconds.

▲ **Hot and cold**
The muted grays of this industrial scene contrast with the fiery hues of the gas flare and the sky.

LOOK IT UP!
Panorama p. 64–65
Montage p. 66–69
Natural light p. 24–25

55 mm focal length

▲ **Perfect harmony**
The striking colors of the truck and the bridge, the sky and the river, all harmonize together.

▶ **Same position, different views**
The advantage of having an SLR camera, or a compact with a good zoom lens, is having a range of lens focal lengths to choose from so you can achieve a variety of viewpoints. The series of pictures on the right were taken with a zoom lens set at different focal lengths. The photographer pivoted the camera around from the same position to record a visit to a local park.

▲ ▲ ▶ Changing light

The direction and quality of the light striking your subject can completely change its appearance. Here is the same mountain shot at different times of the day. The first picture was taken early in the morning and shows the sun illuminating every detail of the mountain's craggy surface. The next shot was taken in late afternoon, with mist diffusing the sunlight and creating a more moody picture. In the final picture, taken at dusk, the mountain is backlit and appears as a silhouette against a dramatic, late evening sky.

70 mm focal length

90 mm focal length

210 mm focal length

PANORAMAS

SOMETIMES a scene can be so wide that you have to turn your whole body to take it all in. It can be quite a problem to capture a view like this on film. If your camera has a wide-angle lens or zoom setting, and you stand far enough back, you might just about fit the whole scene in. But on the print, the details will be so small that the picture will lose its impact.

A professional photographer might have a special panoramic camera for situations like this. The lens on this camera swivels as it takes the picture and produces a very long negative. But you can get the same effect by taking a series of pictures from the same spot and putting them together afterward. This is called a panorama. You will need to support your camera, or use a tripod, to keep the camera steady. You can even make a picture that covers 360° – a complete circle.

▲ ▶ Wide-angle comparison
This single picture (above) was taken with a wide-angle 28 mm lens. Although it takes in a lot of the scene, it doesn't capture the whole sweep of land as in the panoramic version (top right). The wide-angle lens also makes the subject details look small and unimpressive.

Image 1

SHOOTING A PANORAMA

Choose a panoramic scene to photograph, then find a level surface, such as a wall or post, which you can use to steady the camera.

1 *Position the camera for your picture. Take the first shot, then swivel the camera to the next part of the scene. Include a slight overlap, as this will act as a guide when you put the prints together. Repeat to cover the complete scene you are photographing.*

2 *When your prints are returned, match up the overlaps to recreate the view. Carefully glue the prints together. You can either trim the tops and bottoms or leave them in "steps," like the ones shown on these pages.*

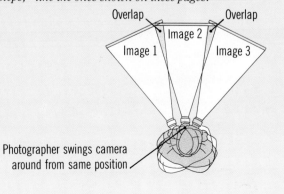

Overlap   Overlap
Image 2
Image 1   Image 3

Photographer swings camera
around from same position

▼ Urban view
This canal scene is framed by trees and bushes, which give scale and depth to the picture.

▼ Grand scene
A panorama captures the whole of this stunning view of the Grand Canyon.

ap   Image 2   Overlap   Image 3

MONTAGE

A SIMILAR technique to panorama is montage. This sort of photographic compilation is a bit like a jigsaw puzzle. Instead of just joining photographs together in a long strip, you make a patchwork of pictures. These will cover both the length and depth of the scene. The advantage of this technique is that it shows a much wider area of picture than a panorama.

There are no rules with montage. You can simply mount the finished prints on a piece of stiff cardboard for display, trimming the edges to fit a frame, or leaving them to make an interesting irregular shape. You can wait until you have assembled your prints, to see which suits the subject best.

HOW TO SHOOT A MONTAGE

1 Stand in one spot and take your photographs in a systematic way to ensure you cover the whole scene.

2 To avoid gaps in the finished montage, overlap adjoining areas that contain important details.

3 Leave out areas such as broad expanses of cloudless sky, but keep the horizon as it provides continuity.

4 Assemble your finished prints. Overlap the pictures to cover the length and depth of the scene.

▲ **Distorted view**
In this montage, featuring details of a fishing boat, the photographer was not trying to create a recognizable, real-life subject. Parts of the scene, like the mast and crow's nest, were repeated many times, but each was shot from a slightly different angle.

▲ **Split image**
This unusual montage was made from a single photograph of a Chinese pagoda. It was then cut into pieces that were rearranged to create an interesting abstract image.

▼ River estuary
This montage takes a panorama one step further by adding more depth and height to the river scene.

◄ Modern architecture
For this montage of office buildings, the photographer shot from close-up, far away, and from different angles. Modern architecture offers many opportunities for dramatic montage pictures, as the repeated shapes can be easily distorted by moving the prints slightly out of line.

▲ Group montage

In order to include a long row of people in the same shot, a professional photographer might use a special camera with a lens that rotates as it takes the picture. You can get a similar effect and add depth to your scene by carefully taking a series of photographs and joining them together. If you look carefully at the picture above, you can see that the same person has been included at both the beginning and the end of the group. This adds an extra touch of humor.

MAKE A FRAMED MONTAGE

You can only see a few pictures at a time if you mount your prints in an album. If you have a collection of prints, perhaps of a special occasion or group, you can create a montage that can be framed to hang on a wall. This type of montage is made up of many separate prints, each with its own complete image. Photographs taken on vacation, at home, and at Christmas time and other occasions all go to make an interesting and a varied montage.

1 *Collect pictures with different backgrounds, colors, and views to give variety. Position your first picture roughly in the middle of the space.*

2 *Arrange the other images around your first one. As you can see here, these pictures will start to define the overall shape of the montage.*

Subjects positioned
in a circle

Direction of
camera swing

Arrange your subjects in a circle around you, as shown here. Stand in exactly the same spot, but swivel to take each picture. In this way your subjects will always be the same distance from the camera. When the shots are joined together, the group will look as if they were standing in a row.

▶ **Facial montage**
An unusual idea for a montage is to take pictures of the faces of each member of your family. Join details from each person together to make a single picture or family portrait.

4 *When the montage is assembled and you are happy with all the pictures, lift each one carefully, apply glue, and press into position. The finished montage in this example has been framed, but you could pin the pictures onto a bulletin board.*

3 *Now you can start filling in the gaps. It doesn't matter if pictures overlap, as long as you are careful not to cover up any important details.*

STILL LIFE

STILL life photographs are of objects, not people or places. There are no rules about which objects to use, but those that have something in common – such as color, texture, or shape – often work well together. You will find that even the most ordinary things make good subjects.

Rearrange the objects you select until you are happy with the way they look. You will have to experiment with different lighting and camera angles to get the best results. The background of your subject is also very important. Choose a setting carefully so that it complements the subject, but doesn't distract the eye.

Indoor set-up

Most still life photography is done on a convenient surface (right) such as a tabletop. The objects to be photographed are placed on a piece of colored or white background paper, which is bent upward behind the subject to create a single, continuous surface. The main light source is natural daylight coming in through a nearby window. A reflector has been used on the far side of the objects to reflect some of the window light back into the shadows and lighten them a little. The camera is mounted on a tripod. This leaves the photographer free to arrange the objects and check the composition through the viewfinder.

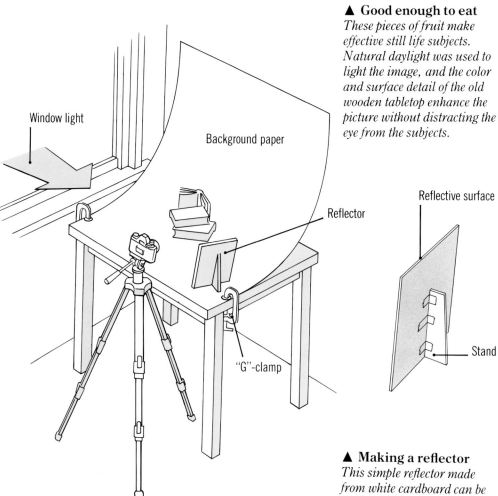

Window light

Background paper

Reflector

Reflective surface

Stand

"G"-clamp

▲ **Good enough to eat**
These pieces of fruit make effective still life subjects. Natural daylight was used to light the image, and the color and surface detail of the old wooden tabletop enhance the picture without distracting the eye from the subjects.

▲ **Making a reflector**
This simple reflector made from white cardboard can be used to reflect light and direct it into areas in shadow.

▲ Flower power
For a dramatic image, make your subject fill the frame. In the picture above, tight framing emphasizes the vibrant colors of the flowers, which were lit by natural light from a window.

◀ ▼ ▼ Tabletop tips
These three pictures were all taken using the simple tabletop setup shown on the opposite page. All of the arrangements fill the frame without looking cluttered. For the colorful close-up (below left), a macro lens setting was also used.

LOOK IT UP!
Reflector p. 90
Macro lens p. 90
Depth of field p. 21, 43, 88

Discovering a still life

You can find interesting arrangements of objects almost anywhere – around your home, out in the garden, or in the street. These make perfect ready made setups for still life shots. Look out for interesting patterns, contrasting or harmonizing colors, or a collection of complementary shapes. In some cases, you might want to make minor alterations to the arrangement, but you will find many subjects that don't need any rearrangement at all.

▲ Fallen apples
You can crop an image to suit the subject. Here the picture shape echoes the line of the garden tools, leading your eye down to the apples at the bottom of the picture.

▲ Autumn leaves
The two photographs above reflect the feel of autumn. The rusty metal in the top picture blends with the muted autumn shades. The mass of color in the picture below provides a perfect background for fallen leaves.

▲ Color contrasts
The bright primary colors of this ball contrast with the dull greens and browns of the background setting.

LOOK IT UP!

Composition p. 22–23

Close-ups p. 76–77

Natural light p. 24–25

Subjects everywhere

Look for potentially interesting still life subjects. Shop windows are always a rich source, as shopkeepers arrange their goods to appeal to the passer-by. Display stands are often full of repeated shapes and bright colors. Even bicycles, propped up and awaiting their owners' return, can make an unusual composition.

SPECIAL EFFECTS

WHEN you take pictures, you usually want your finished prints to look as much like the original subject as possible. But you can use special effects to enhance an image, or make it look visually interesting rather than immediately recognizable. Many effects can be achieved simply and without any extra cost. For others, such as color changes, you may need to buy special attachments for your camera.

◄ **Mirror magic**
This clever special effect was achieved by photographing a reflection, rather than the neon sign itself, in the mirrored glass wall of a building.

▼ **Using patterned glass**
The photographer took this intriguing picture through the type of heavily patterned glass you often find in a front door. The subject, although very distorted, is a pathway and gate.

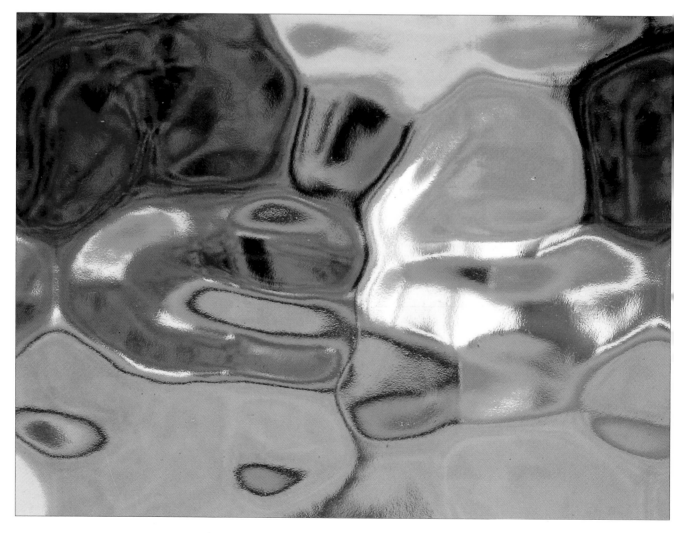

Effects with filters

Soft focus

You can buy special soft-focus filters that have a grid of very fine lines engraved on their surface. However, you can achieve a similar effect simply by stretching a piece of stocking material over the lens itself or over an ordinary UV filter.

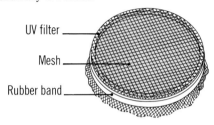

UV filter
Mesh
Rubber band

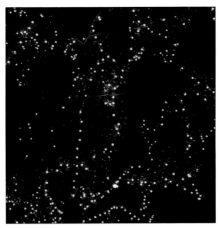

▲ **Christmas lights – without filter**
Before the filter is added, the lights, although distinct, have little impact.

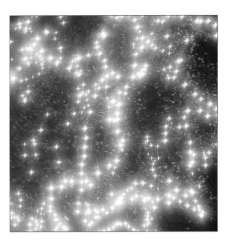

▲ **Christmas lights – with filter**
Stocking material stretched over a UV filter creates a soft, blurred effect.

Smeared image effect

For an image that is very obviously distorted, smear petroleum jelly over plain glass or a UV filter. The more jelly, the more distorted the result. Never put petroleum jelly on the glass of the lens itself.

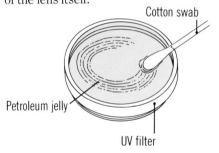

Cotton swab
Petroleum jelly
UV filter

▲ **Flowers – without filter**
Without the filter, this is a very attractive still life of sunflowers.

▲ **Flowers – with filter**
A jelly-smeared UV filter makes the flower look as if it were rotating.

Special effect filters

Gelatine special effect filters are inexpensive to buy. A wide range of effects are available, including many different colors, some with a clear center spot and others that graduate from dark to light. You need a filter holder to attach the filter to your camera lens; these are available for SLRs and compacts. Handle gelatine filters carefully. They are fragile and soil easily.

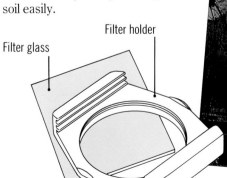

Filter glass
Filter holder

Tobacco-colored filter

75

CLOSE-UPS

THE great thing about close-up photography is that you can reveal a subject, or part of a subject, in a way that may never have been seen before. One of the best places to practice this technique is at home. The most ordinary of subjects can look mysterious or intriguing when viewed very close up.

You cannot focus most compact cameras on a subject that is closer than a few feet from the camera. To take very close shots, you will need to use an SLR or compact camera that has a macro lens setting to magnify your subject. The objects used for the close-up pictures on these pages are everyday kitchen utensils. They are shown in the photograph below.

CLOSE-UP PHOTOGRAPHY

Camera

Cable release

Tripod

Subject

Many modern lenses have a macro setting. This allows the lens to focus closer to the subject than usual. Depth of field is always extremely shallow when taking close-ups, so you will need to select your smallest aperture to increase the zone of sharp focus. Using small apertures usually means selecting a slow shutter speed to compensate (unless the subject is very bright and you are using a fast film), so a tripod is essential to prevent camera shake. Firing the shutter with a cable release will enable you to release the shutter without jarring the camera.

▲ Odd ones out
Can you spot the objects in this picture shown in close-up on these pages?

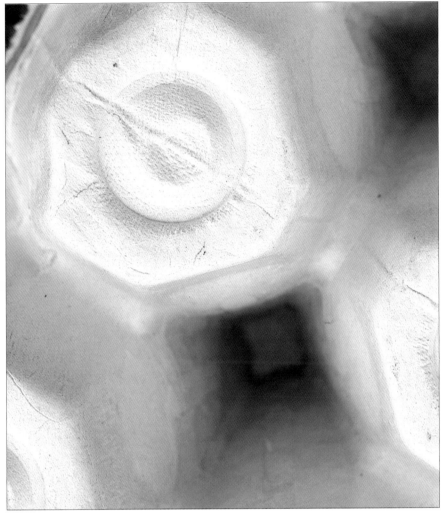

◄ ▼ ▼ ▲ Strangely familiar
As you can see from these photographs, by concentrating on a particular part of an object in close-up, you can draw attention to texture, shape and color. Unusual camera angles and lighting effects will add impact to your pictures.

LOOK IT UP!

Cable release p. 16

Macro lens p. 90

Tripod p. 91

Abstract designs p. 78–79

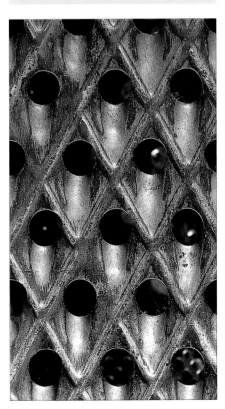

ABSTRACT DESIGNS

THE key to abstract photography is looking at objects in a totally different way. Rather than photographing the whole object, an abstract view usually highlights or emphasizes one aspect, such as color, texture, or pattern, by concentrating on a detail. You will find subjects in the most unusual places, but you will have to look very carefully. Industrial areas in particular are full of great photo opportunities.

PHOTOGRAMS

A photogram is a print made directly from the subject itself, and is produced by placing objects on top of a piece of printing paper and exposing them to light. You will get a more even image if you use an enlarger, but you can use natural light, although the finished photogram will not be quite as sharp.

Step 1
If you are working in a darkroom, place a piece of printing paper on the enlarger baseboard, emulsion side up, and arrange your objects on its surface. If you are using natural light, place your objects on the paper in complete darkness.

Step 2
Set the enlarger lens to about f8 and give an exposure of 15 seconds, or expose the printing paper to natural light. Where the objects block the light, the paper stays white, where the light reaches the paper, it will turn gray or black.

Light source

Subject

Photographic paper

▲ **Road reflections**
Tight framing has turned this night-time reflection of neon lights in the wet surface of a road into a luminous dazzle of abstract color.

▶ Crumbling paint

▶ **Crumbling paint**
Moving in close has isolated this small section of crumbling paint and the underlying brick. Setting the camera at an angle has helped to emphasize the picture's abstract qualities.

LOOK IT UP!
Making a print p. 30–31, 88
Photographic paper p. 30
Close-ups p. 76–77
Special effects p. 74–75
SLR equipment p. 16

▲ **Rough rope**
You can almost feel the rough texture of this rope, which is highlighted by the sun.

▼ **Splash of color**
A detail of a metal door splashed with paint provides an interesting contrast of colors and textures.

SELF-PORTRAITS

TAKING self-portraits can be a lot of fun. There are several techniques you can use, but for most you will need to put the camera on a firm surface, or use a tripod. You can use a self-timer if you have this facility on your camera. The ten second delay after you press the shutter-release button gives you time to position yourself. Alternatively, use a cable release, which is an extension cable that triggers the shutter. This will also enable you to stand away from the camera, and still take a picture. Other techniques are using a mirror and holding the camera at arm's length.

▲ Clowning around
A self-portrait doesn't have to show you as you appear every day. The use of costumes can change your image.

▲ Cyclist friends
You don't have to leave yourself out of group shots. The photographer joined the cyclist group in this picture by using the camera's self-timer.

SELF-PORTRAIT SKILLS

● Position the camera on a convenient flat surface, and look through the viewfinder. Make sure you are happy with the surroundings you've selected.
● Autofocus cameras are easy to use for self-portraits. But you must make sure that you stand in the target area (this is usually in the middle of the viewfinder).
● With a manual camera, prefocus on an object that is the same distance from the camera as you will be when the picture is taken.

▲ Feet first
A self-portrait doesn't have to include your face. The subject of this picture is the photographer's own feet, as seen from a sitting position.

◄ **Dramatic lighting**
This picture was taken using a cable release (seen in the photographer's hand). A sunbeam acts as a spotlight, leaving much of the picture in shadow.

LOOK IT UP!

Natural light p. 24–25
People portraits p. 38–41
Cable release p. 16
Self-timer p. 90
Parallax error p. 20

▼ **Using a prop**
Although this is a self-portrait, by holding a second camera as a prop, the photographer has made the picture appear as if it were taken by somebody else.

◄ **Mirror image**
If you are using a mirror to take a self-portrait, the camera must be mounted on a tripod, or supported, because you will need to use a slow shutter speed to compensate for the lack of light. If you don't want the camera to appear in the picture, put it at an angle to one side of the mirror, out of the shot.

DISPLAYING
YOUR PICTURES

Y OU have taken lots of photographs. You may even have developed and printed some of them yourself. But unless you display your pictures, no one else will be able to enjoy them. There are lots of ways you can present your pictures. The simplest way is to put them into albums. This will also protect your pictures and keep them clean. Keep a different album for each subject. If you frame your prints, either in store-bought or homemade frames, you can hang them on a wall. But remember that you don't need to frame the whole of a picture; you can crop it to give the image more impact. This section of the book shows you how to use L-shapes to choose a suitable section of the print. Finally, you will find information on how to take your interest further – through courses, exhibitions, books, and magazines – plus some useful addresses for further information on different aspects of photography.

PICTURE PRESENTATION

Y OU will soon build up a collection of
photographs that you are proud of. There
are lots of ways you can display them. This
makes them easier to view and allows other
people to enjoy them, too. Photo albums are
useful for storing lots of pictures and for
carrying them around. Your favorite prints can
be enlarged and framed, or you could even turn
them into greetings cards for family or friends.

Enlarged print album

Flip album

Self-adhesive, spiral-bound album

Types of photo albums

Photo albums come in all shapes
and sizes, from small pocket types
to large, book-sized albums that can
hold up to a hundred prints. Some
albums require corner mounts,
others are self-adhesive with a
protective plastic top sheet that
holds the prints securely in place.
Enlarged prints have more impact,
and special albums are made for
prints of up to about 8 x 10 in
(20 x 25 cm) (far left). The range of
albums for the various sizes of print
include this handy 80-picture
flip-up design (top left) as well
as large-format albums with
rigid pages (below left).

FRAMING WITH L-SHAPES

To decide exactly which part of your
picture you want to frame, cut two
L-shaped pieces of cardboard, like
those shown here.

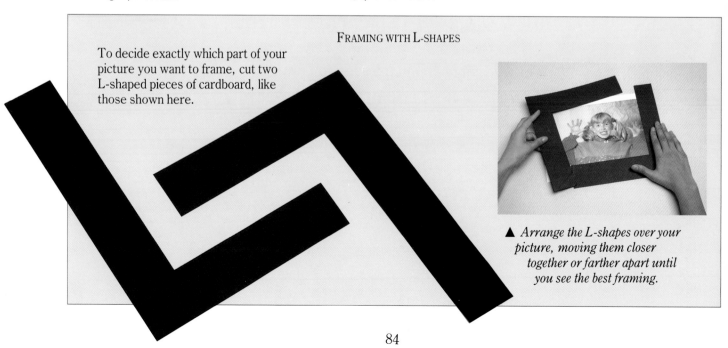

▲ *Arrange the L-shapes over your
picture, moving them closer
together or farther apart until
you see the best framing.*

Making a photocard

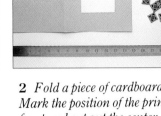

1 *Gather together all the materials and equipment you need to make and decorate your photocard, together with the print you intend to use.*

2 *Fold a piece of cardboard in half. Mark the position of the print on the front and cut out the center of the card to make a frame.*

3 *Attach the print to the inside of the card frame with tape or glue. Now your card is ready to decorate.*

4 *Decorate your card frame with anything you wish. Use a color or a decorative theme that complements the picture, or suits the occasion.*

◄ **Photocard ideas**
Photocards are a fun way to use your pictures. You can use them for any occasion. Decorate your cards with anything you like to give an interesting design. Wallpaper and wrapping paper are useful. You can even add glitter and stickers.

Mounting and framing

You will find a huge variety of ready-made frames in stores. They vary in price and quality, as well as size. You can also discover very attractive antique frames if you visit second-hand shops. But whichever frame you choose, careful and accurate mounting will make your picture look even better.

◄ ▲ Frame styles

These are a few examples of the many different frames that you can buy. They range from those with fancy cast metal borders to simple plastic clip frames.

FRAMING A PRINT

1 *Have an adult help you to trim your print neatly with an X-acto knife and a metal ruler.*

2 *Turn the print face down and place strips of double-sided tape at regular intervals across the back of the print. Trim off any excess tape.*

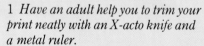

3 *Cut a piece of mounting board to the size of the frame you are using. Peel the backing paper off the tape and carefully place the print in position.*

4 *Smooth the print down so that it is perfectly flat. Place the mounted print on the backing board, and position the glass on top. Clip them all together.*

Many schools have photography clubs that you can join. This will give you access to school photographic facilities and a darkroom, as well as provide you an opportunity to further your learning with other people who share your interest. If there isn't an established club, why not form your own? Talk to your art teacher or a member of staff who is interested and willing to help. Some school districts or local groups offer evening classes, although these may have age restrictions.

You can go on to college or a university to study photography at a higher level. This is generally the way to start if you want to become a professional photographer.

Photographic exhibitions

Many cities have photographic exhibitions at regular intervals during the year. Some galleries specialize in photography and present continuous exhibitions of different photographers' work. One such museum is the International Center of Photography in New York City. The center has locations at 1133 Avenue of the Americas as well as at 1130 Fifth Avenue. Keep an eye on your local newspaper for other exhibitions.

Books and magazines

There are many well-written and beautifully illustrated books on photography. Some concentrate on the technical side of the subject, others on aesthetics. Try your local library, which should have a section on photography. You could save up for any books that are particularly useful or perhaps ask your parents for them as birthday presents.

Magazines are another excellent source of information. Magazines such as *Popular Photography*, Petersen's *PHOTOgraphic, Practical Photography, Camera*, and *American Photo* can provide inspiration and ideas for your own shots. Many of the magazines provide information on the latest in photographic equipment. Some publish announcements of photographic competitions, with various categories of entry to suit different age groups and subject matter. If you are eligible and feel confident about some of your photographs you might want to enter.

Useful addresses

The Photographic Society of America (PSA) publishes a monthly journal which you might find useful. The society can be contacted by mail at: 2005 Walnut Street, Philadelphia, PA 19103. There are a number of other organizations, some of them very specialized.

Some photographic organizations include:

Professional Photographers of
   America, Inc.
1090 Executive Way
Des Plains, IL 60618

The American Society of Media
   Photographers
14 Washington Road, Suite 502
Princeton Junction, NJ 08550

Office of Photographic Services
National Gallery of Art
Constitution & 6th Street, NW
Washington, D.C. 20565

National Press Photographers
   Association, Inc.
3200 Croasdaile Drive, Suite 306
Durham, NC 27705

International Photographers'
   Association, Inc.
2063 N. Leavitt
Chicago, IL 60647

GLOSSARY

A

Abrasions
Long, straight scratches running down the length of a film. This type of problem usually occurs if there are tiny particles of grit on the film pressure plate of a camera. Each time you advance the film is dragged over this grit and so the scratch becomes longer and longer. To prevent this, clean the film pressure plate before loading each new film into the camera.

Abstract image
An image that is nonrealistic, usually concentrating on an aspect of a subject, rather than the subject as a whole. This is often achieved by photographing just a small part.

Angle of view
The amount of a scene that can be taken in by a lens, also called lens coverage. A wide-angle lens has a wider angle of view than a telephoto lens.

Aperture
The opening behind the lens, usually within the lens barrel, that allows light into the camera to expose the film. The size of the opening can be made smaller to allow less light in when light levels are high, or larger to allow more light in when light levels are low.

Autoexposure
An automatic system, also called automatic metering, found on most modern cameras. It adjusts the aperture size and the shutter speed to ensure correct exposure.

Autofocus
An automatic system found on many compact and SLR cameras. It adjusts the focus setting of the lens to produce a sharp image.

B

Backlight compensation button
A control found on some cameras that opens the lens aperture up to allow extra light into the camera when the subject is lit from behind. This compensates for the fact that the side of the subject facing the lens will be in shadow.

Backlighting
A type of lighting effect that occurs when the subject is positioned between the sun and the camera.

C

Camera obscura
An early drawing aid. Originally a darkened room with a tiny hole in one outside wall. Light entering the room through the hole would project an upside-down image of the scene outside onto the opposite wall. This image could then be traced onto paper or canvas.

Compact camera
A small, highly automatic camera with a lens that cannot be removed and changed for another. The viewfinder is separate from the lens.

Contrast
The difference between the brightest and darkest parts of a picture.

Converging verticals
A trick of perspective that makes vertical parallel lines seem to converge as they get farther away from the camera.

Cropping
Changing the camera position or the focal length of the lens to select certain parts of a scene. You can also crop in on a negative when making a print, or crop a print by cutting or mounting it.

D

Darkroom
A lightproof room where film is processed and prints are made.

Daylight-balanced film
Color film that is designed to give accurate subject colors when exposed by daylight or by flash.

Depth of field
The zone of sharp focus in a picture. Depth of field varies depending on the lens aperture, the lens focal length, and where the lens is focused. Small apertures have a greater depth of field than large ones; wide-angle lenses have a greater depth of field than telephoto lenses; and depth of field becomes greater the farther away the lens is focused.

Developer
A processing chemical used with film and printing paper that converts the invisible image, present in the photographic emulsion, into an image that can be seen.

Diffused light
Light that has passed through some type of semi-opaque material, such as tissue paper or gauze, and been scattered.

E

Emulsion
The light-sensitive coating on film or paper that records the image of the subject. The emulsion consists of crystals of silver halides mixed with gelatine.

Enlarger
The piece of equipment used in a darkroom to make enlarged prints from film. It has its own light source and lens, and projects an image of the film down onto a baseboard where the printing paper is positioned.

Exposure
The amount of light received by a piece of film or printing paper. In a camera, exposure is controlled by a combination of the aperture size and the length of time the shutter remains open (the shutter speed).

F

Fast film
Film that is very sensitive to light and is used when lighting conditions are dim. Fast films have large ISO numbers, such as ISO 1600 or 3200.

Film clip
Weighted clips that are attached to the top and bottom of a roll of processed and washed film so that it can be hung up to dry. The weight prevents the film from curling as it dries.

Film pressure plate
A sprung metal or plastic plate on the inside surface of a camera's back. When closed, this presses the film perfectly flat before exposure.

Filter
A glass disc, or a piece of plastic or gelatine, that fits over the front of a camera lens and is designed to alter the color or appearance of the image.

Fixer
A processing chemical, also called hypo, that makes the remaining unexposed silver halides on film or paper soluble. This means that they can then be washed away, leaving the film insensitive to light.

Flash
A portable form of artificial light used mainly indoors, at night, or when there is not enough light outdoors for a successful exposure. Many compact cameras have a built-in flash, but SLR cameras usually need a flash unit to be attached.

Floppy disk
A magnetic disk that stores information. In a still video camera, the disk records the different intensities and other characteristics of the light rays entering the lens. When the camera is linked to a television set, the disk displays full-color pictures.

Focal length
A lens measurement describing the distance between the back of the lens and the film. A lens that has a long focal length, such as a telephoto lens, increases the size of the image in the frame. A lens with a short focal length, such as a wide-angle lens, decreases the size of the image in the frame. Focal length is usually measured in millimeters.

Focusing
Moving the lens either closer to or farther away from the film in order to produce a sharp image.

F stop or f number
One of a series of numbers engraved on the control ring of a lens. They indicate the size of the lens aperture. Moving to the next largest f number (f8 to f11, for example) makes the aperture smaller. Moving to the next smallest (f5.6 to f4, for example) makes the aperture larger.

I

Image
A photographic representation of a real scene or object.

ISO
An abbreviation for International Standards Organization. An international system for rating the speed of film.

L

Large-format camera
A type of camera used mainly by professional photographers. They produce pictures on large individual sheets of film, which are loaded into the camera one at a time.

Large-format film
The individual sheets of film used in a large-format camera.

Lens
A single piece of specially shaped glass, or a series of pieces of glass, that focus the light rays entering the camera onto the film.

Lens hood
A cup-shaped attachment, made from rubber or metal, that fits around the front of a lens. Used mainly on SLR cameras, this prevents bright light, usually the sun, from shining directly into the lens and causing flare.

Light meter
A light-sensitive device in a camera, linked to both the lens aperture and the shutter, that controls the film exposure. In non-automatic SLR cameras, the meter displays aperture size and shutter speed recommendations for the photographer to set manually.

Light rays
In photographic terms, these are the individual "parts" of light energy that radiate from every point of a subject. Light rays that enter the lens are bent, or refracted, so that they come into sharp focus precisely where the film is located, forming an image on the film.

L-shapes
A framing device made from two L-shaped pieces of dark colored cardboard which allows you to preview how the final photograph will look.

M

Macro lens
A lens designed to allow closer-than-normal focusing so that extreme close-up pictures can be taken.

Macro setting
A lens setting found on many SLR zoom lenses and some compacts. This allows the lens to focus on a single point that is closer than the normal focusing range of the lens.

Microprism collar
A focusing aid found in the center of the viewfinder of many SLRs. It is a shimmering circular band that clears when the lens is correctly focused.

N

Negative
A film image showing dark areas of the subject as light, and light areas as dark. In a color negative, the colors will also be reversed. When printed, subject tones and colors appear normal.

O

Overexposure
The result of too much light reaching the film, giving a very light, bleached print.

P

Panorama
A picture made by taking overlapping images of a scene and then putting them together to give a longer picture than would otherwise be possible.

Pentaprism
A five-sided prism inside an SLR camera. This corrects the inverted image so that it appears the right way around in the viewfinder.

Photographic (printing) paper
Paper coated with a light-sensitive emulsion, designed to reproduce a positive print from a film negative. Black-and-white printing paper is available in both resin-coated and fiber-based types. Resin-coated paper has a barrier under the emulsion that prevents chemicals and water from penetrating the paper itself. This makes processing and washing times much shorter than with fiber-based types, which become saturated. Although fiber-based papers take longer to process and wash, and tend to curl when drying, they do produce richer blacks and cleaner whites than resin-coated papers, so many photographers prefer them.

Photojournalism
Telling a story using pictures. Captions may be added but the photographs are the most important part.

Polarizing filter
A gray-colored filter that, when fitted over the camera lens, removes some types of reflection, such as those from glass windows and the surface of water. It also tends to strengthen the color of blue skies and so increase the contrast between sky and clouds.

Print
The standard, album-sized enlargement that is produced by most automatic processing and printing machines.

R

Reel
A plastic or stainless-steel spiral-shaped device that holds an entire roll of exposed film. Once the film is loaded onto the reel, it is inserted into a developing tank containing processing chemicals. The shape of the reel ensures that the coils of film are kept well separated from each other so that the chemicals can reach all parts of the emulsion.

Reflector
Any material, such as a piece of white cardboard, that reflects light onto the subject. Reflectors are usually positioned opposite the light source to reflect light back onto the subject, lightening the shadowy areas.

S

Safelight
A special red light that is used when making black-and-white prints. Black-and-white photographic printing paper is not sensitive to this color, so you can work in the darkroom with some light on.

Self-timer
A control button that delays the shutter release. This gives the photographer time to run around in front of the camera and be included in the picture. On most cameras, the delay is 10 seconds.

Shutter
A lightproof barrier, either in the lens or inside the camera body, that opens to allow light entering the lens to reach the film. The length of time the shutter stays open can be varied depending on the exposure needed by the film.

Shutter-release button
A control button found on all cameras. When pressed, the shutter opens, allowing light from the lens to reach the film.

Slide
A film image that shows subject tones and colors correctly. Prints can be made from slides, but usually they are meant to be projected onto a wall or screen for viewing. Slides are often called transparencies.

Slow film
Film that reacts more slowly to light and is used when lighting conditions are bright. Slow films have small ISO numbers, such as ISO 100 or 200.

SLR
An abbreviation for single lens reflex. This type of camera has a lens that can be taken off and changed for another. An angled mirror inside the camera body reflects light from the lens up into the viewfinder, so that you always see the subject as the picture will eventually look.

Split ring
A focusing aid found on some SLR cameras. When the image is properly focused, the two halves of the image within the ring match. When unfocused, they do not.

Sprocket holes
Holes running along the top and bottom of 35 mm film. Inside the camera, the film advance system has tiny "teeth," which fit into the holes and move the film forward and backward from cartridge to take-up spool.

Squeegee tongs
Plastic tongs lined with pads of foam rubber, used to remove excess water from processed film.

Standard (or normal) lens
On a 35 mm camera, this is a lens with a focal length of about 50 mm. It is called a "normal" lens because the angle of view, or amount of a scene it takes in, is about the same as you would see with the naked eye. A lens with a shorter focal length is known as a wide-angle; one with a longer focal length is called a telephoto.

Stop bath
A processing chemical used in the darkroom to process film and printing paper. It halts the action of developing solution.

T

Telephoto lens
On a 35 mm camera, this is a lens with a focal length greater than 50 mm. Telephotos have a narrow angle of view and fill the frame with a small area of the subject. Telephoto lenses are very useful for sports, nature, and candid photography.

Test strip
A strip of printing paper that has been subjected to a range of different exposures. These are produced either by altering the size of the aperture of the enlarger lens or, more usually, by altering the length of time the enlarger is switched on. A test strip may contain, for example, exposures of 5, 10, 15, and 25 seconds. Once it is processed, you can see which exposure time is best, and then make an enlargement of the entire negative using this exposure.

Tripod
An adjustable, three-legged stand with a platform on top, which holds the camera securely. You usually use a tripod when you need to keep the camera really steady, such as with a slow shutter speed.

U

Ultraviolet (UV) filter
This colorless lens filter helps to remove excess amounts of UV light, which is often seen as a haze in the distance on landscape scenes and in coastal regions. Because it is colorless, many photographers leave a UV filter on the camera to protect the delicate front surface of the lens.

Underexposure
The result of too little light reaching the film, and producing very dark prints.

V

Viewfinder
The sighting device of a camera, which allows you to aim the camera lens accurately at the subject and to choose which parts of the subject will appear on the print.

Viewpoint
The position or angle of the camera when taking a photograph. Slight changes in camera viewpoint can make large differences to the appearance not only of the subject itself but also of its surroundings.

W

Wetting agent
A few drops of wetting agent, added to the final washing water of processed film, prevents droplets of water from forming on the surface of the film as it dries. Without it, such droplets can stain or mark the film.

Wide-angle lens
On a 35 mm camera, this is a lens with a focal length shorter than 50 mm. These lenses have a wide angle of view and take in a broad area of a scene, but the subject detail will look very small. They are useful lenses for panoramic scenes, and when working in cramped spaces where you can't move very far back from the subject.

Z

Zoom lens
This is a lens with an adjustable focal length, such as 28–70 mm or 70–210 mm. It can be used to produce a range of effects.

INDEX

Bold type indicates the main subject headings.

M

macro lens 23, 48, 71, **76**
magazines 87
microprism collar 21
microscope adapters 16
mirrors, using 81
montage 66 – 69
mounting 86

N

natural light 24 – 25, 40, 60, 70, 78
nature photography 48 – 49
  see also animal photography
negatives 28, 29
Niépce, Nicéphore 12

O

110 cameras/film 14, 18, 19
overlapping frames 34

P

panning 44, 45, 62
panoramas 14, 56, 64 – 65
panoramic cameras 62
parallax:
  error 20
  marks **20**, 32
people 38 – 39, 40 – 41, 52 – 53
  see also action photography,
  sports photography
personal view 52 – 53
photo albums 84
photo story 54 – 55
photocards 85
photograms 78
photographic exhibitions 87
photography clubs 87
photo-journalists 54
pinhole pictures 12
pivoting the camera 45, 62
point of focus 22, 23
Polaroid cameras 17, 18
portraits:
  of animals 42 – 43
  of people 38 – 39
  posed 38, 53
  self- 80 – 81

using flash 27
printing paper 30, 31, 78
print tongs 30, 31
prints 18, 19
  displaying 84 – 86
  framing 86
  making 30 – 31
processing errors 35
professional cameras 17

R

red eye 35
reflection 51, 74
reflector 40, 70

S

safelight 30
self-portraits 80 – 81
self-timer 80
shadows 24, 25, 60
sharp focus 21, 76
sheet film 18
shutter 12, **13**
shutter-release button 12, 13, 20, 80
shutter speed **21**
  and camera shake 32
  and close-ups 76
  and mirrors 81
  and moving water 61
  and sports/action photography 44,
  45, 46
silhouettes 25
silver halides 12, 19, 28
single lens reflex cameras *see*
  SLR cameras
slide film 18, 19
slow film 18, 19
SLR cameras 13, **15**
  using 21
soft-focus filter 75
special effects 74 – 75
split-ring 21
squeegee tongs 28, 29
still life 57, 70 – 73
still video camera 17
stop bath 28, 29, 30, 31
support, using a 20,
  and camera shake 32
  and panoramas 64
  and portrait shots 38
  see also tripod

T

telephoto lens 15, 16
  and animal/nature photography
  43, 48
  and camera shake 32
  and people photography 38, 39

35 mm cameras *see* compact
  cameras, SLR cameras
timer 29
transparency film 18, 19
tripod 62, 64, 70, 76, 80, 81

U

useful addresses 87

V

vacation photography 56 – 59
viewfinder **12**, 13, 15, 80
  in compact cameras 20
  in SLR cameras 21
viewpoint **22**, 23, 46, 47
vignettes 33

W

water, photographing moving 61
waterproof case 16
weather 24 – 25, 60
wetting agent 29
wide-angle lens 15, **16**
  and animal photography 42
  and buildings 50
  and panoramas 62

Z

zoom lens 15, **16**
  and animal/nature photography
  43, 48
  and panoramas 62
  and people 38, 39, 56